★ ★ ★ ★ ★

the

RUDE PUNDIT'S
almanack

LEE PAPA

0/
/R

OR Books, New York

© 2011 Lee Papa

Visit our website at www.orbooks.com

First printing 2011.

Cover and interior design and layout: A. Galperin
Illustrations (pgs. 13, 55, 77, 88, 109, 114-15, 169, 178): Jennifer Kimball

Library of Congress Cataloging in Publication Data:
A catalog record for this book is available from the Library of Congress

British Library Cataloging in Publication Data:
A catalog record for this book is available from the British Library

Printed by BookMobile, USA

The printed edition of this book comes on Forest Stewardship Council-certified, 30% recycled paper. The printer, BookMobile, is 100% wind-powered.

paperback ISBN: 978-1-935928-42-3
ebook ISBN: 978-1-935928-41-6

10 9 8 7 6 5 4 3 2 1

★ ★ ★ ★ ★

the **RUDE PUNDIT'S** almanack

LEE PAPA

illustrations by
JENNIFER KIMBALL

OR Books, New York

CONTENTS

DISCLAIMER:
All labels and titles are rhetorical. Just because I call someone a "motherfuck-er" does not mean that I have firsthand knowledge that that person fucks his or her mother. However, I do not have knowledge that he or she does not fuck mothers. Additionally, simply labeling someone a "cocksucker" does not imply any knowledge that the person sucked any cock. Should that person by chance suck cocks for pleasure or profit, it is purely coincidental.

NOTE:
My helpful researcher, Kristina Montesano, was not paid nearly enough for the soul-crushing work she did. She should consider this her letter of recommen-dation for any graduate program.

INTRODUCTION

This book is unfair, and I am imbalanced. Of course, I have drugs that take care of the latter, the pole for the delicate tightrope walk of chemicals in my brain, although tequila is probably flicking the cable a bit. As for the unfairness? Well, at least I'm honest. I'm not presenting this as the truth (even if it is) or a corrective to a mostly conservative media. No, this almanac is a chronicle of our accelerating descent into madness in this America, and it's an attempt to toss out an anchor, put on some brakes, or at least claw the earth with our fingernails to try to stop our plunge off the cliff.

The results of the congressional elections of 2010 were a warning sign: if you dance with the capitalist devil, you are going to get burned. The Republican takeover of the House of Representatives and the GOP gains in the Senate, as well as in gubernatorial and state legislative races were the next act in a passion play for our democracy that is being scripted to near-perfection by corporations. This occurred in the wake of the *Citizens United* decision in the Supreme Court, which said, in essence, corporations can anonymously pour cash into elections because they have the same speech rights as real people.

And the Tea Party and all their teabaggage? That was merely playing the buffoons and yokels for everything they're worth. For what is the end result of their "ideology"? A modified anarchy? A Frito-Lay-sponsored oligarchy? It is that each of us should have the right to squat in our shitpiles of ignorance, isolated from one another, coveting our precious money, fellating our guns and fucking ourselves against our 50-inch LED screens in our multi-mortgaged, soon-to-be foreclosed on hovels, and if the world outside our caves goes to hell, well, that's because people don't understand how wonderful it is to engorge your faces with poisoned food and asthmatically heave your chest through polluted air and travel on shattered roads and bridges while picking your unmedicated scabs in order to get to work at Wal-Mart for shit wages. If that's the America you want, then give it another couple of years.

But it ain't mine. No. It's not America as I learned it to be. They want a confederacy of loosely-affiliated states who only come together in order to have a military defend them from the big, bad outside world. I want a more perfect union, united states, if you will.

I was born in Rego Park, Queens. When I was just barely out of toddler pants, my first girlfriend was the daughter of a member of the Argentinean ambassador's staff. When we left in a hurry one day, on the run from the law (or so my grandfather said when he was in dying delirium), she stood on the sidewalk and waved goodbye as we pulled our Chrysler away from the curb and headed down to Florida, where we ended up living in a mobile home, on welfare, while my father worked as a bartender at some Coconut Grove-type place and then as a semi driver for Eckerd Drugs. We didn't think of ourselves as rednecks, even though we lived in a trailer park and my mom paid for groceries with food stamps. No, we thought the Gieselman family next door from Ohio (truly, King's Manor was a refugee camp for Union exiles), whose patriarch sat on the porch of his double-wide and chewed tobacco and who we called "the Spitters," were the rednecks. I had been to a movie premiere at Radio City Music Hall. My brother had been photographed with various Yankees and Mets. It takes years to accept that one's been downgraded from solidly middle class to working class. It takes years to get back to solidly middle class. And that was when you actually had a good shot at doing it.

I tell you all of this not as some way of getting across my man-o'-the-people street cred or to give you some bullshit *Christmas Sweater* sob story. You don't really know anything about me.[1] I'm not gonna sit here and go into the various jobs I had in warehouses or weep about my dad dying when I was 13. No, fuck that. I'm telling you this because I want you to understand that when I write this shit, I'm writing from a dual position: I have a PhD and I know how to catch crabs with chicken necks.[2] I'm not some Northeastern-raised, Ivy League liberal for whom the day-to-day existence of the masses is theoretical or transient (like a summer job in the Ozarks or some such shit). I don't have access to people in power any more than any other American. I've met a few, but Al Franken ain't gonna return my calls. I'm just a guy who's been at it for a long time, over 25 years, staying engaged and watching the raft go over the falls. More than anything, I'm probably someone whose funhouse mirror image is something like the Tea Party. But with longer hair.

So this book is a bit of a journey, of how one gets to be a raging, unapologetic liberal after coming out of the trailer and into the light. All it takes is a little bit of attention to the people, to the news, and to the world you walk though every day.

Let's set a few ground rules. As far as I'm concerned, there's a few things that we need to believe without question, things that aren't even up for debate and won't be debated or justified here:

---

1 I don't mean you, Mom.
2 Full disclosure: My degree is in English, not history or political science. My dissertation was an examination of American drama and the history of unions and workers in the early twentieth century. Majoring in English in the late twentieth century meant you learned how to interpret a text and how to "read" the world around, say, a poem or novel. When you apply those skills to the speeches of Sarah Palin, the cognitive dissonance would make a robot go on a city-burning rampage.

- Abortion should be safe and legal. The only regulations should be those that keep it safe and legal, like other legal medical procedures.
- Global warming is real and happening because of human beings.
- Gay people should be allowed to get married because, really, nothing is going to stop it from happening. In fact, whatever the country deems legal for straight people to do, that's gotta be legal for the GLBT community.
- Barack Obama was born in the United States.
- The presidency of George W. Bush (with the aid of Congress) is the reason why the nation is in its current dire straits. The greatest success of the right has been to pin the failures of the Bush administration on Barack Obama.
- Fox "news" is biased in a way that the New York *Times* or CNN or even MSNBC could never hope to be.

But even if you take a few things off the table, even if you think some issues are just obvious, you need to know what the left is up against. Here's an actual Facebook wall "conversation" I had with an old friend in August 2010 over the immigration policies of the Obama administration, especially as it regards a memo that discussed the possibility of the President issuing an executive order of amnesty for illegals:

ME: Are you aware that the Obama administration is deporting illegals at a higher rate than any other administration? And that, in fact, the number of people crossing the border has gone down because of the actions of Barack Obama? Or do facts just not matter?

JASPER[3]: You've been reading the Daily Kos again, haven't you?

ME: Nope. (Followed by a citation of a *Washington Post* article that gave exactly how many people were deported.)

JASPER: Those articles are a JOKE. That's why Fox "news" and Newsmax aren't running them!!

ME: Hey, wow, look at this AP story I found on the Fox "news" website

3 Not his name. But calling him "Jasper" will just annoy him. That makes me laugh.

(or do they just republish liberal lies now?). (Followed by a link to said article.) Jasper, numbers are numbers. These are facts. Facts are indisputable. It's why they're facts. You can use them to prove your point, but the actual facts don't change.

JASPER: The FACTS, Lee, are that Obama and his minions are attacking businesses that DO NOT EMPLOY ILLEGALS because they either can't speak English and/or they don't have the skills to work in the industries being targeted now. The mainstream media publishes factually inaccurate stories all the time because they automatically accept this regime's statements at face-value without verifying anything they say.

ME: Where are you getting your info? I mean, I don't quote Daily Kos to you. Are you quoting Newsmax or WND to me? Because those are as biased as any left wing blog. Show me how every news organization is lying. Prove it to me.

JASPER: The only people lying here are Obama and his regime. The problem is that people like the ones who work for the New York Times, Washington Post, CBS, et al, take EVERYTHING these assholes say as gospel and refuse to vet and or verify ANYTHING.[4]

Jasper and I went for a while until I got sad and gave up.

This is what the left is up against. Here's how many layers of bullshit and denial that we have to plow through. It's the kind of delusion that led to the Republican resurgence. But even if this book ends up just preaching to the converted, that's okay. The converted go to church. They deserve some preaching so they can go out and transform themselves and the world around them. So come on in to the chapel. Maybe bring a friend. The wine's good. And when we get down to flesh eating, well, let's just say that some metaphors are a whole lot more fun than others. ⓡⓟ

---

4 The sad part is that I don't completely disagree with Jasper. The media helped create the Iraq war. And during the Bush administration, I complained about how the media became merely the transcribers for the White House. But the denial of plain facts is stunning.

★
★
★
★
★
★

Part 1:

JANUARY, 2009

I WAS THERE. Goddammit, I was there. Sure, there are about two million people who can say as much, probably millions more who would claim so. And my friends in Fairfax, Virginia, whom I was staying with, were shocked that I decided to go. But I froze to be there. I know what we all thought, what we all >

believed that January 20. I know how the air crackled with expectation. I know what it all meant. The crush of people in my area of the National Mall on Inauguration Day 2009 made us seem less like individuals than a single surging, gigantic organism. If someone five bodies behind you leaned forward, you leaned forward. Human heat made us warm on that almost sarcastically cold day. Yet there was virtually nothing but elation, a gathered nation ready to welcome an instantly transformative moment. Indeed, if you think about it, there, in that moment, this was what America was poised to become after September 11, 2001, had the former administration decided to harness the power of unity. But then again, it was never very good with alternative forms of energy.

Everyone released purgative, cathartic boos at George W. Bush and Dick Cheney. The television coverage may have muted it, but it was there. A young woman half-heartedly said, "Oh, c'mon, y'all, that's mean," but she cracked up when I said, "Sometimes a man deserves to be booed by a million people." The most touchingly surprising crowd reaction was the cheer that went up for Jimmy Carter. Most everything else was as expected: the too-respectful quiet for porcine preacher Rick Warren, tears as Aretha Franklin sang, the nearly unbearably joyful roar when Barack Obama took the oath of office, understanding that, however badly Chief Justice John Roberts screwed it up, it was real. People began to drift away as poet Elizabeth Alexander read her actually quite good poem, and they snapped back to attention when the Rev. Joseph Lowery called out old 1960s chants about racial harmony, all, all a way of saying, "We've finished a chapter. Let's write the next one."

On the Metro ride into town, in the crowd itself, and in the streets afterward, the diversity of celebrants was kind of staggering: the family wearing "Filipinos for Obama" buttons (who, fortunately, looked Filipino), the older white guy wearing a Human Rights Campaign hat and Obama buttons with the rainbow flag across them, the two guys walking on Independence Avenue with scarves that had "Palestine" on them, so many of the disenfranchised now thinking they were, at least, welcome in answer to one big "Thank you."

And the sheer number of black people: the jubilant families on the Metro, the giddy students around me on the Mall, the older men who simply said to each other, "I wasn't going to miss this." I've been in large audiences of black people before, at gospel churches and festivals, but I've always sensed a divide, like, for some at whatever event, I was a kind of interloper, a spy, even. That's my damage, my whiteness giving way to my own suspicions. But not on that day. I've never seen such a seamless connection between black and white, as I watched, for instance, white suburban women chatting up and laughing loudly with middle-aged black women. When Obama spoke, it was with the idea that we all did this, that it couldn't have been done any other way, and that we very much needed each other as we turned from the jubilation to the journey.

One part of the story you might not have heard: As a way of letting people warm up from the gut-twisting freeze, which hit me immediately after the crowd started to disperse, all of the museums of the Smithsonian were opened so we could have a place to rest for a little while. The one that was closest to me was the Museum of Asian Art, and I staggered in, needing to just sit, drink something, and breathe in air that didn't feel like small knives in my lungs. Walking past ivory carvings and tapestries and watercolor paintings, past the galleries with floors filled with people, like I was wandering through the fanciest refugee camp in the world, I found an open spot near a display of samurai armor. I leaned against the wall and sank down, opening my black wool coat and taking out a bottle of water. It hit me just how many rules were being relaxed for this day. Bag and coat checks seemed cursory, beside the point. No one cared about all the people who had squatted there, eating and drinking. It felt, for lack of better words, so old-fashioned.

Or maybe just communal. The woman next to me offered me Teddy Grahams that she had been giving to her son. We all started sharing stories of where we had come from to be there, why we had come, what we had done during the campaign, where we had stood in the crowd. There must have been twenty of us in that corner near the swords and armor, and all around the gallery, all around the museum, and, I presumed, around all the museums, people were doing the same. I'm not someone who idealizes people or events, but sometimes, you know, to state something is "ideal" is just to state what you're actually observing. Isn't this what democracy was supposed to be like? Citizens actually giving a damn about the day-to-day running of the nation?

I sat there for nearly an hour, and then I thought for sure that the crowds must have lightened up for the ride on the train. I tucked back in and headed into the cold, only to learn a quick lesson in crowd dynamics when the number of people was larger than I had ever seen. There was nothing to do but jump on the wave and ride.

A young black woman and her mother were walking with the tide of humanity. The young woman was talking about how some of her friends thought she was crazy to go out into the cold when she could have easily watched it on TV. "No way," she said, "I wanted to be there for my president. I wanted to answer him when he made that call to work." And he had told us he would. Obama had told us that he would need us on this new road we were digging out for ourselves.

All around the Capitol, after the event, increasingly desperate button hawkers were trying to sell "I Was There" pins. Nah, I thought. I knew where I was. I know where I am.

I know how that energy is almost all used up now, how the weight of expectation, the burden of history, the unexpected sharp turns of events and economy, the trashed state of the nation have burned it up like so much lamp oil. Barack Obama never made that call for us, the millions who wanted him elected, to come back and work some more. He didn't tell us what to do with that newfound civic energy. It was misdirected and abused by others, transformed into things like the Tea Party, or otherwise it was drained or washed away, as we became numbed by the sun coming up and the actual amount of devastation left behind by the Bush administration became clear. Goddamn, it might have been better just to shutter the joint up and ask Canada if we could join.

No, no, though. We wanted to work, that day, and the days after, even if the odds were against us. Even if there was too much to do, even if it's taken years to fill the hole where the World Trade Center used to be while the Pentagon is back to normal. Even if every good thing Obama does is compromised and mitigated and undercut by war and politics and circumstance. We are delusional, yes, we Americans, delusional enough to stand on frozen earth so we could hope for the hope and change. Yet, despite having one of the most successful first terms in office ever for a US president, it feels as if Obama failed us and we failed him. And such moments as we the people seem further and further away. ⬤

AFTER THE PARTY

ON JANUARY 28, 2009, a couple of days after I got back from DC, I wrote the following:

"We don't know what Barack Obama actually said to Republican members of Congress in his closed-door meetings with them yesterday regarding his stimulus >

plan. But we do know one thing for sure: It accomplished nothing. This is the way it's gonna go, and if you've paid attention at all, you know the steps: Obama will concede shit and Republicans will ask for more (even though they already got more tax cuts than anyone fucking needs), Obama will concede more shit and Republicans will ask for more (even though they're gonna get the family planning funding taken out), Obama will concede more shit and Republicans will ask for more, and then when the vote comes, Republicans will vote against it, saying that no one listened to them and fuck that Obama for lying about bipartisanship. Yet the legislation will have passed in a watered-down form...

"Obama better know a simple fact: They fucking hate him. Right now, Obama represents the knowledge that everything they believed was a complete failure. For making that clear to the American people, they fucking despise him. They hate his majority, they hate his coattails, they hate that all over the country people are supporting his ideas. Republicans have nothing right now, which means they have nothing to lose by trying to drag Obama into their pit of shit. They'll smile and say it was a good conversation, but they're waiting in the back halls of the Capitol to fuckin' shiv Obama and laugh while he bleeds. And try to force Americans back into their crooked arms."

In that one blog post, I was more right than William Kristol,[1] editor-in-chief of *The Weekly Standard*, has been in his entire career. **;P**

---

1 One should always and forever be reminded that Kristol ran Alan Keyes's campaign for president.

SAME SCRIPT, DIFFERENT DECADE

From *Time* magazine, January 27, 1936, the script of an actual radio ad from the Republican Party:

MARRIAGE LICENSE CLERK:
Now what do you intend to do about the national debt?

PROSPECTIVE BRIDEGROOM JOHN:
National debt? Me?

CLERK:
You are going to establish a family and as the head of an American family you will shoulder a debt of more than $1,017.26—and it's growing every day... Do you still want to get married?

JOHN:
Well—er—I—I—What do you say, Mary?

MARY:
Maybe—maybe—we better talk it over first, John... All those debts! When we thought we didn't owe anybody in the world.

JOHN:
Somebody is giving us a dirty deal... It's a low-down mean trick...

VOICE OF DOOM:
And the debts, like the sins of the fathers, shall be visited upon the children; aye, even unto the third and fourth generations!

(Music).

HOW TO MAKE SOMETHING COMPLETELY INNOCUOUS APPEAR TOTALLY EVIL

SOMETIME IN THE MIDDLE OF 2009, in an effort to carve a pentagram into every single thing the Obama administration attempted, some conservative think tanks and commentators, most prominently Glenn Beck, began attacking the White House for the number of >

"czars" it had employed. Depending on who is counting, the number has varied somewhere between thirty-two and forty-five czars working for the president. However, if you were asking, say, Peter the Great, these upper-mid-level bureaucrats would seem significantly less czar-ish and more like "employees."

What constitutes a czar is up for debate, since many of them are executive office staff with sinister titles like "Assistant to the President for Science and Technology" (in this case, John Holdren, who is called the "Science Czar" but not, for instance, by John Holdren, his bosses, or anyone who works for him). Those kinds of positions have always been at the whim of the president, since he does have to hire over 1,500 people to run the joint. But some of the czars are also approved by the Senate, like the Director of the Office of Information and Regulatory Affairs, who in this administration is Cass Sunstein, or, really, the "Regulatory Czar."

In other words, if you can take a word from the person's title and put czar after it, then, like magic, that person becomes a czar and is thus a great deal more evil than they ever thought they would be.

Now, the right likes to insist that the number of czars increased exponentially in the administration of George W. Bush, and even more so under Obama. They say that Ronald Reagan had only one, a Drug Czar. But that's only because there's only one person Reagan ever referred to as a *czar*. And commentators weren't so loose about handing out those labels randomly. In fact, if we apply the same standards to Reagan's appointees that are applied to Barack Obama, well, he had way more than one czar.

DIRECTOR OF THE OFFICE OF INFORMATION AND REGULATORY AFFAIRS, or, as it's currently known, "Regulatory Czar":
   1983: *Douglas Ginsburg*

SPECIAL REPRESENTATIVE TO THE MIDDLE EAST, or "Middle East Czar":
   1982: *Philip Habib*
   1983: *Donald Rumsfeld*

SPECIAL ASSISTANT TO THE PRESIDENT AND DIRECTOR OF THE ADVANCE OFFICE, or "Scheduling Czar":
   1981: *Stephen M. Studdert*

SPECIAL ASSISTANT TO THE PRESIDENT FOR NATIONAL SECURITY AFFAIRS, or "National Security Czarina":
   1981: *Janet Colson*

SPECIAL ASSISTANT TO THE PRESIDENT FOR INTERGOVERNMENTAL AFFAIRS, or "State Legislature Czar":

> 1981: *Judy F. Peachee*

SPECIAL ASSISTANT TO THE PRESIDENT AND DIRECTOR OF THE 50 STATES PROJECT FOR WOMEN, or "Chick Czar":

> 1982: *Thelma Duggin*

SPECIAL ASSISTANT TO THE PRESIDENT AND ASSISTANT DIRECTOR OF COMMERCE AND TRADE WITHIN THE OFFICE OF POLICY DEVELOPMENT, or "Some Kind of Trade Czar":

> 1982: *Wendell Wilkie Gunn*

SPECIAL ASSISTANT TO THE PRESIDENT "TO ASSURE THAT POLICY ANALYSES FOR THE PRESIDENT ARE SENSITIVE TO THE NEEDS AND PRIORITIES OF THE MINORITY AND DISADVANTAGED COMMUNITIES," or "Negro Czar":

> 1982: *Melvin L. Bradley*

SPECIAL ASSISTANT TO THE PRESIDENT FOR DRUG ABUSE POLICY, or "Best Czar Job Ever":

> 1983: *Carlton E. Turner*

SPECIAL ADVISER TO THE PRESIDENT AND SECRETARY OF STATE ON ARMS CONTROL, or "Peacenik We Ignored Czar":

> 1984: *Paul Nitze*

SPECIAL ASSISTANT TO THE PRESIDENT FOR LEGISLATIVE AFFAIRS, or "Senate Ass-Kicking Czar":

> 1985: *Frederick D. McClure*

By the way, this list only contains those people Reagan himself appointed

Beck also includes people who were appointed by others, such as the Assistant Secretary of Homeland Security. That's right: In our current hysterical climate, someone who was appointed by a cabinet member, who herself was confirmed by the Senate, has now been elevated to the level of czar.

What sounds evil and anti-democratic is almost always just spin and lies, nothing but spin and lies. **₨**

SOUTH CAROLINA SENATOR

Jim DeMint

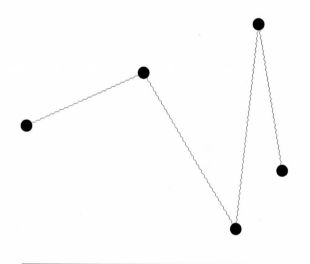

Jerry Falwell's bitch

David Koresh's gun polisher

Father Coughlin's best altar boy

Jim Jones's Kool-Aid mixer

Cotton Mather's wig brusher

1999　2000　2001　2002　2003　2004　2005　2006　2007　2008　2009　2010

continues on following page >

ANALYSIS OF POSSIBLE REPUBLICAN PRESIDENTIAL CANDIDATES

SOUTH CAROLINA SENATOR

Jim DeMint

continued

1999: Voted to ban gay adoption in Washington, DC. Voted for a flag-burning constitutional amendment.

2004: During his campaign for Senate, DeMint said that he wanted to ban openly gay teachers from schools in South Carolina: "If a person wants to be publicly gay, they should not be teaching in the public schools." He later apologized for "distracting from the debate."

2008: Hates fucking of all kinds not between two married heterosexuals of different sexes: "Of course, the best sexual education is happening in homes. There is no substitute for parents discussing this issue with their kids. But if sexual education is going to be taught in our schools, it should be focused on abstinence only. Unlike other approaches, this one actually works." He'd be right if he wasn't wrong.

2009: Co-sponsored, with every extreme-right bag of nuts in the Senate, a bill that would apply the Fourteenth Amendment to fetuses: "the terms 'human person' and 'human being' include each and every member of the species *homo sapiens* at all stages of life, including, but not limited to, the moment of fertilization, cloning, and other moment at which an individual member of the human species comes into being," which means he thinks that all birth control, all morning-after pills, and more ought to be banned.

2010: Demonstrating a fine understanding of the science of climate change, DeMint tweeted, "It's going to keep snowing in DC until Al Gore cries 'uncle.'" Also became de facto head of Senate Teabagging.

☞ PREDICTION

Jim DeMint will run through at least the South Carolina primary, at which point the rest of the nation will realize that he's from South Carolina. No chance at all of winning the nomination, but he has a small chance of being some moderate's nutzoid vote-getter as a vice-presidential candidate.

Part 2:

SPRINGTIME FOR REAGAN

When I was thirteen, I asked my mother to take me to see William F. Buckley speak. That's right, the clenched-teeth motherfucker who started *National Review*, great goddamned godfather of modern conservatism, and me, impressionable, young, thinking that anyone who was on TV had some >

worthwhile authority, not realizing what scumsuckers these people could be. And I was so frigging full of myself, so wanting to make an impression on Buckley, as if he would pluck me out of the crowd and say, "Yes, you shall be my scion. Have some money and a patrician accent that sounds like you desire yachting off the Vineyard." The speech took place at Blackham Coliseum in Lafayette, Louisiana. I'm not joking when I say that a week prior to Buckley's appearance, there had been a rodeo there. And I'm not above saying, in retrospect, that it makes sense that the man who opposed the Civil Rights Act would talk in an actual pit of bullshit.[1]

Buckley spoke for about an hour and then asked for questions. You had to ascend stairs to a microphone that was a good distance from him. I had written down my question beforehand, scrawled on the back of an envelope in the car. I dutifully waited my turn, nervous as hell, and I walked up to the microphone after not having understood a thing he had said all evening. I glanced at my crumpled envelope and asked, "What advice would you give young people about what we can expect in the future?" Not profound, but I wanted to bond, you know? I was thirteen. What was I going to do? Ask him about the economic underpinnings of underground capitalism in the Soviet Union?

And after a goodly round of guffaws at my question from the gathered bourgeois coonasses at how oh-so-fuckin' precocious I was, Buckley swerved his fused-spine neck around in my direction and said, "Well, I'm not a psychic," which got orgasmic cries of laughter from the crowd, most of whom probably hadn't understood him either but were too ashamed to admit it and too smart to actually get up and ask a question. Then I tuned out while he said something about Adam Smith and income tax rates and really, who the fuck cares? I received patronizingly polite applause when I left. My first encounter with evil. And not too many scars.

Hell, I got off easy. My family's got a picture of Richard Nixon holding my brother when he was a kid. Sometimes, when he gets in a pool, you can still see on his chest and stomach the acid slime marks from Nixon's fingers. ℞

---

1 To be mildly fair, Buckley later said he regretted that opposition. But that didn't help back in 1965.

Founding
Fathers
Fun Time

GLENN BECK on his radio program, July 18, 2008:
> "I didn't like the way the HBO John Adams special portrayed Franklin, as a real womanizer. There is absolutely no evidence, there is not a single letter, there's not a single... There's no evidence of that, none whatsoever."

In his *Autobiography*, part 1, written in 1771, published in 1793, BENJAMIN FRANKLIN says that he loved hookers and feared the syph:
> "[T]hat hard-to-be-governed passion of youth hurried me frequently into intrigues with low women that fell in my way, which were attended with some expense and great inconvenience, besides a continual risk to my health by distemper, which of all things I dreaded, though by great good luck I escaped it."

**I TOUCHED
RONALD REAGAN AND HAVE THE
SCARS TO PROVE IT**

WHEN YOU'RE THIRTEEN YEARS OLD, you don't know any better. You might think you do, but, really, if you're not allowed to drive, you don't know any better. So it was that I heard on the news that Republican presidential candidate Ronald Reagan was going to be having a meet-and-greet at the Lafayette >

Regional Airport. This would be sometime in about April 1980. All I knew was that someone who might be in the White House was coming to our town. No, wait, that's not entirely true. The real, whole, "oh, shit, okay, I'll just confess it" truth is that I wanted Reagan to be president. All I knew was media hype and what my parents had to say. And they wanted Reagan, too.

I begged my Mom to take me to the airport. She agreed, because are you going to say "No" when your child says, as I did, "This is a chance to see history"? We headed out in our huge, bright green Chevy Malibu station wagon with ripped seats, a company vehicle for my Dad, over to the small airport in our town of about 50,000 people back then. Lafayette Regional was mostly used for helicopters transporting workers back and forth for their seven days on and seven days off the oil rigs out in the Gulf of Mexico.

My parents, who had voted for John Kennedy and Nixon, were hard to pin down politically,[1] although my father was a racist homophobe from the Bronx who fancied himself something of a Waylon Jennings–listening shitkicker. He was a "when in Rome" kind of guy. Among the books we had around the house, the author who was second only to Agatha Christie and just ahead of Peter Drucker was the aforementioned William F. Buckley. Dad even had me sit down to watch *Firing Line* occasionally, and he'd agree constantly with Buckley. He was on the road several days a week, and his untreated depression left him often incapable of doing fatherly things when he was around. So if being conservative gave me time to hang out with my Dad, then sign me up, man.

The event was held in a hangar, and, this being before we were all such cowards, we parked and walked right into the event. No security shakedown. No lists of approved people. Reagan had finished speaking at a fundraising dinner, and he was coming out to say "Hello" to the crowd before flying away. I had my little 110 camera, and I was blocked from the front of the receiving line, over a velvet rope, by various newspaper and magazine photographers, including this one who had about six huge Nikons hanging around his explorer's vest. I thought, "I want a goddamn picture," and I leaned in and tripped the guy, who stumbled as I pirouetted in front of him. Secret Service wasn't gonna boot an adolescent who was trying to meet the future president. Imagine the spectacularly bad press.

Reagan saw me. I clicked a picture I would love to show you but set on fire when Reagan died. I was this close to the Gipper, the man who I came to

1 My mom later told me that they were registered Republicans until we moved to Louisiana, which was when she changed to "Democrat" in order to vote in a primary. So less devotion than expediency.

despise with a heat that could melt flesh. But at that moment, I was honestly thrilled. It's one of those karmic episodes that I think I've been working off for a long, long time. "Well, hello, there, young fellow," Reagan said to me, sounding just like Ronald Reagan, and he put out his hand, "What's your name?" Of course, I shook it. Of course, I told him my name. At that point, all I could think was how much this was gonna make a hell of a story for everyone back at my eighth grade class, maybe even get me a chance to touch Mary Broussard's tits.[2]

I can tell you this, though, and it is a sensation that has stayed with me since that day. That fucking hand was cold. And the skin felt as if it could tear like tissue paper. I was honestly afraid to squeeze, because I thought I'd hurt him. I was repulsed, as if a walking corpse had just infected me. But I tried to push that out of my mind.

The next day at school, my social studies teacher didn't believe me. She was kind of a cunt, a faded Southern belle who said things like, "I would have rather been a slave than an immigrant. All you had to do was work all day and then you'd have a place to sleep and get some food." She finally acknowledged that I wasn't lying when I got the pictures. I gave one to her. She framed it and hung it on the wall. Until the day she retired, fifteen years later, she kept that godforsaken thing up there. And every year, even as the color faded on the print, she'd tell a new class of students that I was the one who took it.

So, in November 1980, Ronald Reagan was elected. A week later my father would be dead. A month later, so would John Lennon. Even then, I knew bad omens when I saw them. The year ended badly. We were fucked. But I wouldn't realize just how fucked for four years. **RP**

---

2 It didn't.

INDIANA REPRESENTATIVE

Mike Pence

Gary

As devolved as Muncie

As depressed as Anderson

As depressing as Terre Haute

As ugly as Fort Wayne

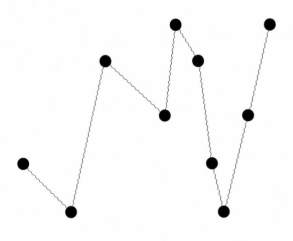

1959: Born in Indiana.

1992: Said, "I'm one of those Republicans who reject the notion that the key to resurgence at the national level is to retreat from the basic values that brought Ronald Reagan to the White House." In Congress ten years later, he would propose "no-amnesty" immigration legislation, just like Reagan. Wait... no, completely the opposite of Reagan.

1995: His conservative radio talker, *The Mike Pence Show*, got syndicated all over Indiana because, certainly, there was no regressive-minded, Christian fundamentalist out there to represent for the people. No, not in Indiana.

2000: Elected to Congress on a campaign of tax cuts and because "We can renew the American dream by rebuilding the military after years of reckless cutbacks, rekindling the fires of men, material, and moral that warm the warriors who stand on liberty's ramparts, protecting our families." Apparently, that made sense to some people.

2001: Secured liberty's ramparts by helping to draft the Patriot Act.

2003: Said of gay marriage: "Numerous studies done in this area confirm what God has always known—that marriage between a man and a woman makes for strong families." God was unavailable for comment. Pence, though, will support a constitutional amendment to define marriage like God wants it defined.

2004: Said, "I am a Christian, a Conservative, and a Republican in that order."

2005: A supporter of the Iraq and Afghanistan wars, as well as unfettered love for Israel and its funding, said of the aftermath of Hurricane Katrina: "Let's figure out how we are going to pay for it. Congress must ensure that a catastrophe of nature does not become a catastrophe of debt for our children and grandchildren."

2007: After securing millions of dollars for his district in his first three terms, he became a vocal opponent of earmarks when Democrats take over Congress.

2009: Wrote an editorial for the disgusting *Human Events* where he calls President Obama a friend to dictators, an "apologist" for the United States, and, generally, weak.

Analysis continues >

INDIANA
REPRESENTATIVE

Mike Pence

continued

☞ PREDICTION

He is from Indiana. He's beloved by
the Family Research Council and is a
smart guy. Chances are he's another
potential vice president to corral the
evangelicals. Or he gets caught in a
threesome with a male midget and a
female horse.

see also

ANALYSES OF *other* **POSSIBLE
REPUBLICAN PRESIDENTIAL
CANDIDATES:**

Jim DeMint (pgs. 17-18), Jeb Bush
(pgs. 30-31), Rick Santorum (pgs.
52-54), Mike Huckabee (pgs. 55-57),
Sarah Palin (pgs. 74-75), Mitt Romney (pg. 78), Newt Gingrich (pgs.
104-105), Haley Barbour (pgs. 126-
127), Tim Pawlenty (pgs. 128-129),
Bobby Jindal (pgs. 169-171)

[NOT]

GREAT MOMENTS IN WEALTH REDISTRIBUTION #1

One of the clearest defenses of raising taxes came from Great Grand Poobah Ronald Reagan during a radio address on November 27, 1982. Reagan described the state of disrepair of America's roads and bridges before proposing a 5-cent-a-gallon tax on gasoline. He called the nearly 4 percent raise a "federal highway user fee," and offered, "The program will also stimulate 170,000 jobs, not in make-work projects but in real, worthwhile work in the hard-hit construction industries, and an additional 150,000 jobs in related industries." Yep, Ronald Reagan wanted to take money from you to create jobs for other people. That son of a bitch.[1]

---

1 By the way, the very idea of holding Ronald Reagan up as a model for anything positive makes me want to throw up my pancreas. Why my pancreas? Because it's deep inside and would hurt like hell.

FORMER FLORIDA GOVERNOR

Jeb Bush

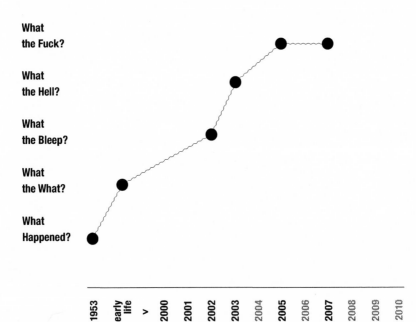

1953: Upon birth, actually saw and touched Barbara Bush's vagina.

Early life: Real name is "John Ellis Bush," so "Jeb" is from his initials. Was called "Jebby" when he was a child.

2002: While governor of Florida, Jebby got his brother, who happened to be president, to buy back the oil and leasing rights on a bit of the Gulf Coast.

Christmas Eve, 2003: Opened the nation's first faith-based prison.

Christmas Day, 2003: The nation's first faith-based prison rape occurs.

2005: Issued an executive order to force brain-dead patient Terri Schiavo to be kept alive for his entertainment, a show that lasted another two years.

2007: By the end of his term, Bush had given tax cuts to corporations and the wealthy to the tune of $20 billion. By 2008, the Florida legislature had to make $3 billion in cuts to the state's budget to make up for a shortfall in revenue.

☞ **PREDICTION**

Believe it or not, Jeb Bush is pretty much the best, if not the only, shot that Republicans have. That says so much about the pathetic state of the GOP that it should make elephants everywhere want to shoot themselves.

see also

ANALYSES OF *other* **POSSIBLE REPUBLICAN PRESIDENTIAL CANDIDATES:**

TWO IN THE BUSH: A CINEMATIC EPIC

Fade in:
Wide shot:

> University of Tennessee-Knoxville campus. It's autumn 1992. The leaves are changing. Students are dressed for slightly cooler-than-normal weather. It's a sunny day.

Cut to:

> A classroom. It's a typical college class, with about twenty-five students of various sizes, shapes, and sexes. There is only one black student. They are bored. Various shots of students talking, staring at books, writing notes. All of a sudden a stocky, but dashing, bearded young professor enters. He is excited.

Medium shot:

PROFESSOR
Hey, I just heard that the president is speaking at the airport in a few minutes. Who wants to go?

MALE STUDENT 1
And not have class?

PROFESSOR
Sure. We'll just write about the experience. It'll be like an assignment.

FEMALE STUDENT 1
I thought you didn't like George Bush?[1]

---

1 The father, not the son. However, the hate remains the same.

PROFESSOR
Either way, it's the president. How often do you get to say you saw
the president speak? C'mon, how many of you have cars?

(A few hands go up.)

PROFESSOR (cont'd)
Then come on! You'll be back by lunch. Let's convoy out there.[2]

(A cheer as bags are packed and people start to head out.)

MALE STUDENT
(Stops walking, to Professor) You're the best teacher on campus.

PROFESSOR
Oh, stop it. Now, let's all meet at the airport!

X-fade to:

*Various shots of students in cars, all heading off to the airport. Shots
of cars on the road. Music montage. Possibly with Guns 'N' Roses
song? Ending with the cars parking at the Knoxville airport and the
students getting out.*

Ext. airport parking lot:

*Professor leads the students into a hangar. They go through security
and end up on the tarmac, heading into the main area near the stage.*
*The stage is festooned with flags, with balloons. Ricky Skaggs
is playing bluegrass. Naomi Judd is standing there.[3] A big crowd is
present on the tarmac and in the bleachers there. The wind is blowing, but it's not too bad. Professor stands in front of the bleachers.*

FEMALE STUDENT
Do we have to stay with you?

---

2 In reality, only about half the class could go, but for the sake of not getting the movie bogged
down in details, let's say everyone went.
3 Naomi Judd is probably 350 years old by now, but we can digitize her to look younger.

PROFESSOR
No, you go wherever you want. But meet back here when it's over.

(Students head out into the crowd. A few stay back near the Professor, who looks almost mythic with his long hair whipping around the breeze and the American flag seemingly glowing behind him.)

Cut to:
The stage. Naomi Judd approaches the microphone.

NAOMI JUDD
Now, I want everyone to put your hands together and give a big Tennessee Volunteer welcome to the forty-first president of the United States, George Bush.

Pan the crowd as cheers go up and "The Star-Spangled Banner" is played.

BUSH
Thank you. Thank you all very much. Before we begin, I'd like us all to join in the Pledge of Allegiance.[4]
(He turns to the flag and begins to recite the Pledge. As he does so, the camera focuses on the Professor, standing with his arms crossed, not pledging at all. A very large young white man in an ill-fitting gray suit and a buzzcut wanders over next to the Professor. He must be over six and a half feet tall. He is saying the Pledge and then applauds when it's over. He glances at the Professor, but listens to the president.)

BUSH
(Says some goddamn thing. Everyone applauds except the Professor. We stay focused on the Professor and the giant standing in front of the flag on the bleachers.)

GIANT
(to Professor) Why aren't you clapping?

PROFESSOR
Sorry?

4 I'm not making this part up. You remember all the bullshit about flag-burning? People actually gave a damn about that kind of cosmetic nonsense.

GIANT
Why aren't you clapping? You should be clapping.

PROFESSOR
(Shrugs) I don't feel like clapping.

(They listen some more to Bush. The Giant continues to applaud with the audience. The Professor listens, but he does not cheer or applaud.)

GIANT
(agitated, in the Professor's face) Why are you here?

PROFESSOR [5]
(thinking, "Oh, shit, this fucker's gonna kill me. But I can't wimp out in front of my students. I hope this doesn't hurt too much.")
What do you mean?

GIANT
(yelling) I said, "Why the fuck are you here?" Huh? You're not clapping. Why not?

PROFESSOR
(not backing down) He's my president, too. I can listen to him if I want.

GIANT
(really in the Professor's face) So why aren't you clapping? Huh? Huh? Why aren't you clapping?

PROFESSOR
(realizing that lingering students are watching now, pissed off) I'm not clapping because that man *(gestures to the stage)* has dragged this country down. And I don't give a shit if that makes you unhappy.

GIANT
(getting ready to swing) You should be clapping, asshole. You should be clapping. That's our president.

[5] This all happened while Bush was continuing to speak. I'd like to think that Karl Rove and Bush, Jr. were over by Air Force 2, giggling and snorting coke and playing grab-ass.

PROFESSOR
Blow me, Gigantor.
(Giant swings right at Professor's face. Cut to slow motion of Professor falling to the tarmac. As the Professor goes unconscious, the screen fades to black.)

Fade up:
Professor is in a hotel room bed. A nude Barbara Bush is laying next to him, staring at him. He wakes up and looks around, confused.

PROFESSOR
What the—

BARBARA
Thanks for the pearl necklace.

(She cackles madly as the Professor screams and credits roll.)[6] ⓡ

---

6 The real story ended a while ago, when Gigantor yelled back at me. Then security came over and told us to knock it off or they'd throw us both out. Gigantor stalked away, presumably to go masturbate into a copy of the Constitution. When the event ended, my students talked about how I stood up to Gigantor. In the end, they remembered that more than the speech. Which is about par for the Bush I presidency.

One of my finest moments?

I was standing in a crowd and Dan Quayle was there. You remember, the guy who couldn't spell potato and became vice president, thus paving the way for the presidency of George W. Bush? Quayle had just finished giving a speech and he was shaking hands, and I thought, as he >

approached me, "I've got one shot. Shit, what can I say that'd mean something to this guy? What can I say that's profound and bone-rattling and beautiful that'll change his heart and turn him into one of us?" And he reached his hand out to me and I grabbed it and he smiled that fake Midwestern smile of "we're all buddies" and I yelled, right in his face, "You're stupid." Total protest fail. Goddamn missed opportunities.

Although I like to think that Quayle went home that night, my words echoing in his empty brain pan, like a slow-bouncing child's ball, and he stared at himself in the mirror, trying to figure out what about him made someone behave so cruelly to him. "My god," I want him to have thought, "am I really stupid?" Then I picture him smacking his head repeatedly, crying out, "Am. I. Stupid?" before rolling around on the ground and yawping like a bear caught in a trap.**ᴿP**

Part 3:

SUMMER OF OUR DISCONNECT

**AMONG THE CHRISTIANS:
FIVE STORIES ABOUT
OTHER PEOPLE'S FAITH**

1. In fifth grade, my neighbor and classmate and red-headed crush, Sarah Logan, was skipping rope right next to where I was climbing on a mailbox. She had been trying to convert me to Jesus for a couple of months, but I wasn't buying. Besides, it was totally more fun to fuck with her about religion >

because she got so fumingly upset if you didn't buy her evangelism. We had been to see the movie *Midway* together and even held hands when the loud planes in the World War II epic at the Plaza Theatre vroomed by on the screen.

As usual, Sarah started talking about Jesus. I don't fully remember what she said, but, surely, it was something about needing to accept Christ as my savior. In shorts, I leapt off my mini-Everest and said, "Sarah, the only thing holy means to me is 'full of holes.'" She clutched the jump rope tightly, no longer jumping, and tears started to sparkle in the corners of her spectacled eyes.

Then she started whipping me with the jump rope on my bare legs, over and over, leaving welts and yelling, "You can't make fun of Jesus! You're gonna go to hell!" Much as it hurt, I almost couldn't stand from laughing so hard as she whipped me all the way to my front door.

2. The Seventh-Day Adventist minister is knocking on the front door of our townhouse. "Stay quiet," my father whisper-yells. And then we hear him walk away, but we don't hear the front gate slam. "He's going around back," Dad says. We adjust our ducked-down positions, and through the curtain of the locked sliding door to the patio, we see the minister, who knocks on the glass and stays there patiently for a few minutes, listening.

Mom, who hates this kind of drama, says, "Just let him in."

Shushing her, Dad whispers, "He'll be gone in a second." But he knocks louder on the glass.

All of this is because Dad wanted us to get a free Bible. We had no Bible in the house, and he thought we should. When he saw the advertisement for the series of "seminars" on God and various cultural issues, with the line "Free Bible if you attend three times," well, this family that hadn't been to a synagogue or church in about five years had all the enticement it needed. We got packed in the station wagon and went to the Holidome that was close to our home just in time for a talk about backwards masking on rock records.[1]

We learned about the evils of not just Judas Priest and Black Sabbath. Oh, no. The Eagles had included Aleister Crowley in the album cover of *Hotel*

---

1 "Backwards masking" or "stupid rock music shit" occurred when a band or artist mixed in a reverse recording of some piece of music or speech to an otherwise normal song. Think the Beatles at the end of "I Am the Walrus" or Prince at the end of side one of the *Purple Rain* album. It's supposed to penetrate your psyche and tell you to do demonic or sinful things that you might not otherwise do. In other words, "stupid rock shit." Sometimes, you couldn't even make out what was sung, but the preacher would tell you, to be sure, if backwards Alice Cooper said, "Eat Mommy's spleen."

California. Electric Light Orchestra was influencing our young, impression-able minds with its light rock psychedelia. And, oooh, didn't that garbled voice sound like it was saying, "Lick Satan's cockknob"?

I bailed on the whole thing at the next seminar, when we discussed mov-ies. The preacher told us that certain films would make us go to hell because they were so filled with satanic imagery and words. He showed us clips of mov-ies that supposedly drove people to murder, although mostly he was just giving us good ideas on how to kill. When it was over, I walked up the mustached, polyester-suit-wearing preacher and told him that I enjoyed horror flicks, like *King Kong* or *Godzilla.* He assured me that he was only talking about movies that seemed to celebrate the Devil, you know, *The Exorcist* or *The Omen.*

I was twelve and had seen *The Omen.* I had liked *The Omen.* This whole mumbo-jumbo Seventh-Day Adventist shit was not for me. And I told my dad as much. Sure, he tried to get me to join him for a third seminar. "That's the last one. Then we get a Bible." I didn't go. He did and we got the Bible.[2]

But the minister, seeing souls—Jewish souls, no less—to save, wasn't about to give up on us. He came over once and hung out, eating dinner with us, pointing out particularly good passages in the New Testament and only the New Testament. Preachers, like stray cats, should never be fed.

So that's how we got here: cowering under the floor while an obsessive preacher stalks us, like a scene out of *Night of the Hunter* or *Poltergeist II.* And I am praying that this man of God will just go away.

3. Let's just say that being the only non-Christian in my elementary school led to moments in my classroom like Ms. Musgrove in seventh grade asking, "So today is the first day of Passover. What does that mean... Lee?" Or "Lee, why don't you sing us the Dreidel song?" I sadly obliged.

4. Let's just say that when you're fourteen and a friend's cousin tells you how he was molested by a priest at his house in Abbeville, Louisiana, you pretty much write off the entire Catholic Church as a worthless force of destruction.

5. The Baptist church in South Knoxville put on a fine Hell House back in 1993. This was before the more famous Hell House of Denver started selling kits so

---

2 I still have that Bible. It's a simple, unpretentious, well-bound copy. It's good for getting the con-text of the occasional reference when I don't feel like looking it up online. What more is needed?

other churches could perform the Christian alternative to a Halloween haunted house. I was utterly delighted to see the ad in the *Knoxville News-Sentinel* that informed us we would learn about the terrors of sin in a trip to Hell. But I thought I needed muscle in case things went badly, so I got my friend Kurt to go along. Kurt was taller than me and had an intimidating dark goatee that made him look like Lucifer. Or a goat.

We arrived after sunset on the cool evening of October 29, not quite peak ghoul time, but you could sense the imminent arrival of ghosties in the crunch of the dead leaves. We headed into the crowded church gym (yes, it had a gym—it's a big-ass megachurch) where teenagers in Freddy Krueger and Michael Myers masks, as well as the occasional hockey mask, à la Jason in *Friday the 13th*, wandered around. I wasn't sure if this was allowed in church because, you know, I'd heard about the evil of horror movies a few years before.

The tickets were just five bucks, and we were sent to sit with a group on the bleachers, where Freddy Krueger would occasionally click his plastic finger blades at us. We were called by a young woman, who asked if we were ready to confront the terrors that awaited us in Hell. Kurt and I were practically schoolgirl giddy with excitement. (IMPORTANT NOTE: This story doesn't end with some lesson in how much we ended up learning or appreciating those who believe different things. Or how the people weren't so bad. There will be no ironic turn in this tale. This is purely "let's laugh at the idiot yokels" elitism because... well, because we're smarter than they are. And it was goddamn funny.)

The first part of the tour was a trip to the unfinished basement. Why I willingly followed a stranger into a dark, underground space, I can't say. I'm just glad I didn't end up in a pit with a poodle and skin lotion. After climbing down several flights of stairs, we reached a dirt path that was lined with black plastic sheeting. Holes punched in it allowed spikes of red light to stream through. People were screaming behind the plastic while a deep voice laughed in the background. I looked at Kurt, who had the biggest grin on his face. This was redneck Disney World, and Space Mountain was just starting.

At the end of the path, the basement opened up into a surprisingly cavernous space, well-fogged by a smoke machine. We moved from station to station and were treated to an array of scenes about the agonies being undergone by sinners who never repented.

Some of the moments were obvious: Sure, an abortion that went that bloodily awry did seem to be a cause for some alarm and probably some charges against the doctor for malpractice. "Wait, is the fetus going to Hell, too?" Kurt asked as the room seemed to be consumed by flames. "It doesn't seem to deserve it."

"Deserve's got nothing to do with it," I said in my worst Clint Eastwood voice.

Other moments were sublimely ridiculous, like the piece titled "Hell, Hell, the Gang's All Here." A bunch of white kids dressed like they had walked out of the grunge costume catalog were all dancing like zombies getting cattle-prodded to music on their headphones that were plugged into their Discmen. It was Nirvana, which is not only satanic, but the name refers to a heightened state of enlightenment in another religion. All of a sudden, "Smells Like Teen Spirit" transformed into a twisted, cacophonous roar as the dancers grabbed their ears and found themselves forced, writhing, to their knees. That didn't help. They went to Hell.

Oh, it went on, with, for instance, the bizarre image of a black teenage boy, covered in cobwebs, standing before a Bible, eyes closed. He represented the person who committed the sin of being bored at church. "Are you fucking kidding me?" I said to Kurt. "You can go to hell because you have a shitty attention span?"

"You probably don't need to worry about it, either way," he answered, and I nodded in agreement, having forgotten what we were talking about.

After the last scene, which was our own condemnation to Hell, we were told to run, run, run to the light at the end of the tunnel or we would be forever cast into the pit of fire. Satan was yelling at us that he was going to get us. We lurched our way up some stairs and, finally, outside into the fresh air. It was a clear dark night, and we were between the back of the gym and the church's large cemetery.

Then I saw where we were being directed. It was a classroom, and we could see someone preaching to the people seated in desks. A very friendly but emphatic woman was telling us to head over to the classroom for the final part of the journey. I looked at Kurt, who said, "You want to go?"

The rest of our group of hell-survivors were already on their way. "I don't think we have to," I muttered. He looked in my eyes, which were indicating the opposite direction. The woman was now telling us to go directly to the light of the classroom to be born again.

We weren't masochists. And, besides, it was almost Halloween. We took off into the graveyard, laughing among the dead. **RP**

ONE GOOD RELIGION STORY

ON A TWO-LANE COUNTRY ROAD, some-fuckin'-where in small town Tennessee one morning, riding with friends after a long night, I encountered a man who looked like Gandalf from *Lord of the Rings* walking alone. After driving past him once, >

we turned around to find out what the hell was going on. Why? Because that's what you do. Because you are human. And when an old man with patchwork robes, long white beard, and a homemade crucifix on a staff crosses your path twenty miles out of any place you've ever heard of, you stop and find out what's going on.

I jumped out of the car and walked up to him. He said his name was Pilgrim George and that he walked the world, that he'd been through forty-one countries, and that he was on his nonstop walking pilgrimage because God had told him to do it. He talks to all who wish, he owns almost nothing, he lives off the kindness of strangers. And then he felt compelled to tell me how he pisses in bushes.

After asking to take his picture, I handed Pilgrim George some money. George asked if we had water, and we handed him two bottles, a cold one from the ice chest and another one for later. He thanked us, blessed us, and went on his way.

In an era when all the fake Christians palm off their violence, their bigotry, and their hateful speech as being a case of God-mind reading, whether it's in shootings at clinics or Glenn Beck trying to convince us of the hellish end times to come, no matter where you stand on religion and gods, it's encouraging to know that a man can put on tire-tread-bottomed sandals and wander the earth in order to ask us to be better people. 🔵

Founding
Fathers
Fun Time

DICK CHENEY on ABC's *This Week*, February 14, 2010
   "I was a big supporter of waterboarding."

GEORGE WASHINGTON, in a 1775 letter to General Benedict
Arnold, regarding the invasion of Quebec:
   "Should any American Soldier be so base and
   infamous as to injure any Canadian or Indian, in
   his Person or Property, I do most earnestly enjoin
   you to bring him to such severe and exemplary
   Punishment as the Enormity of the Crime may
   require."

THE EASIEST TAKEDOWN OF OUR DETENTION POLICY

WHEN IT COMES TO SOME PRINCIPLES, like those enshrined in things like the Magna Carta or the Constitution, you shouldn't care who the hell is in the White House. Here's a basic one: A president should not have the power to >

detain people without charge. On the left, we screamed like banshees who had stubbed our toes during the Bush administration over the imprisonment without charge or trial of hundreds of people at the Guantánamo Naval Base. But that noise has died down considerably since the election of Barack Obama, even though the policy has not really changed, and, in fact, Obama has embraced most of the imperial presidency powers that Bush got a prone-and-willing Congress to give him. Both presidents want you to believe that they should have such sweeping authority simply because you can trust them.

The Bush administration demonstrated, on a nearly monthly basis, why such trust is about as valuable as the information gotten from nearly every person ever kept at Gitmo:

• On January 27, 2002, Vice President Dick Cheney said on ABC's *This Week* with Sam Donaldson: "These are bad people. I mean, they've already been screened before they get to Guantánamo."

• By October 28, 2002, the first four detainees were released.

• On July 17, 2003, in a joint press conference with British Prime Minister Tony Blair, President George W. Bush claimed, "[T]he only thing I know for certain is that these are bad people."

• On July 18, 2003, twenty-seven of those bad people were sent back to their home countries.

(You can see the pattern, here, no? It pretty much continued like that, even into the second term of our Bush/Cheney detour.)

• On June 13, 2005, Vice President Dick Cheney informed Sean Hannity on Fox "news," "The important thing here to understand is that the people that are at Guantánamo are bad people. I mean, these are terrorists for the most part. These are people that were captured in the battlefield of Afghanistan or rounded up as part of the Al Qaeda network. We've already screened the detainees there and released a number, sent them back to their home countries. But what's left is hard core."

• On July 20, 2005, eight hard-core detainees were released or sent to their home countries.

(Even at the end of their years in office, they were insisting that "oh, hey, now it's just really, really bad awful worst o' the worstest people that ever walked the earth.")

• During a December 15, 2008 interview with Jonathan Karl, Vice President Dick Cheney offered, "Guantánamo has been the repository, if you will, of hundreds of terrorists, or suspected terrorists, that we've captured since 9/11. They—many of them, hundreds, have been released back to their home countries. What we have left is the hard core. Their cases are reviewed on an annual basis to see whether or not they're still a threat, whether or not they're still intelligence value in terms of continuing to hold them. But—and we're down now to some 200 being held at Guantánamo. But that includes the core group, the really high-value targets like Khalid Sheikh Mohammed." Despite his self-correction in the first sentence there, he also called them "200 Al Qaeda terrorists" later in the interview.

• On December 16, 2008, three Al Qaeda terrorists were sent back to their home countries.

• On January 13, 2009, Cheney told radio host and gambling man Bill Bennett, regarding the detainees at Gitmo, "Now what's left, that is the hard core." Which, if you're paying attention, is almost exactly what he said to Sean Hannity in 2005, which was over a hundred released detainees ago.

• On January 17, 2009, six more of the hard core were sent back to their home countries. That was just a couple of days before Barack Obama was inaugurated, so did they intentionally release criminals just to fuck with the new administration?

After 9/11, the White House fed us this line about the terrible people we held in a place where they couldn't harm us. Anyone who questioned these actions was called an anti-American terrorist-enabler by the right. Until Hurricane Katrina blew the ski masks off the entire bunch of thugs who ran the country, the mainstream media mostly just went along with the White House line when, right in front of them, was the trickle of released detainees, which demonstrated, conclusively, that George Bush, Dick Cheney, Donald Rumsfeld, Condoleezza Rice, and others were lying. And no one of any authority, like, say, Congress or even just the Democrats, held them to account for it.

Now, not only do we still have Gitmo and Bagram Air Base in Afghanistan (which is a true black hole of detention) but President Obama has claimed the power to assassinate American citizens abroad if "they are trying to carry out attacks against the United States," as one White House official put it. CIA Director Leon Panetta said of one American, "[He] is a terrorist and yes, he's a US citizen, but he is first and foremost a terrorist and we're going to treat him like a terrorist. We don't have an assassination list, but I can tell you this. We have a terrorist list and he's on it." The death penalty is a ludicrous leftover of our barbaric past. The death penalty without trial? Isn't that just called "murder"?

You gotta have some principles. You gotta have some inviolable ways of dealing with the world, no matter who is in charge, or you are a mere spectator to the whims of others.

By the way, on May 12, 2009, talking about Gitmo again, Dick Cheney told Fox "news"'s Neil Cavuto, "The ones that are remaining, about 245, are the hard core, the worst of the worst." At least someone in this world is consistent until the bitter end. ᴿP

FORMER (AND DEFEATED) PENNSYLVANIA SENATOR

Rick Santorum

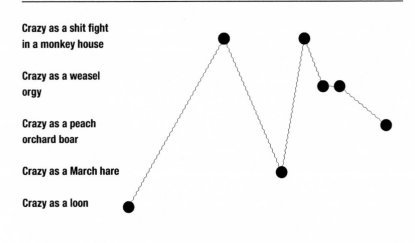

1988: Admitted what everyone knew when, as a lawyer, he represented the World Wrestling Federation in a case to prove that pro wrestling wasn't a sport and, therefore, that its performers could freely use steroids.

1996: Forced his children to play with a dead baby: "In his Senate office, on a shelf next to an autographed baseball, Sen. Rick Santorum keeps a framed photo of his son Gabriel Michael, the fourth of his seven children. Named for two archangels, Gabriel Michael was born prematurely, at 20 weeks, on Oct. 11, 1996, and lived two hours outside the womb. Upon their son's death, Rick and Karen Santorum opted not to bring his body to a funeral home. Instead, they bundled him in a blanket and drove him to Karen's parents' home in Pittsburgh. There, they spent several hours kissing and cuddling [dead] Gabriel with his [living] three siblings, ages 6, 4 and 1 1/2. They took photos, sang lullabies in his [dead] ear and held a private Mass."

2001: Had his by-then five kids in a cyber charter school in Pennsylvania, costing the district there $100,000 over four years, while the Santorum family was actually living in Leesburg, Virginia. Probably paid at least that much in therapy for the youngest three as they attempted to get over being ordered to sing to their dead brother.

2003: Really said, "I have no problem with homosexuality. I have a problem with homosexual acts." Really, really hates gay people. Said in another interview, "In every society, the definition of marriage has not ever to my knowledge included homosexuality. That's not to pick on homosexuality. It's not, you know, man on child, man on dog, or whatever the case may be."

2005: Referring to the Catholic Church sex abuse scandal in 2002 in Massachusetts, he said of Senators John Kerry and Ted Kennedy, "The senators from Massachusetts did nothing. They spoke nothing. They sat by and let this happen." Santorum did not, however, add anything about the church's sex abuse scandal in Pennsylvania at the same time.

2006: Claimed that the revelation that the United States had found degraded, old mustard and sarin gas in Iraq was proof of weapons of mass destruction in that country, a leap that not even the Bush White House would make. Lost reelection.

2010: Says stupid shit all the time on a talk radio show.

Analysis continues >

ANALYSIS OF POSSIBLE REPUBLICAN PRESIDENTIAL CANDIDATES (#4 *of* 11)

FORMER (AND DEFEATED) PENNSYLVANIA SENATOR

Rick Santorum

continued

☞ PREDICTION

Will run for president and fail miserably, will realize that he doesn't have to live in Pennsylvania if he doesn't want to, probably gay.

Please turn the page for the
Analysis of Possible Republican Presidential Candidate
Former Arkansas Governor **MIKE HUCKABEE**

ANALYSIS OF POSSIBLE REPUBLICAN PRESIDENTIAL CANDIDATES (#5 *of* 11)

FORMER ARKANSAS GOVERNOR

Mike Huckabee

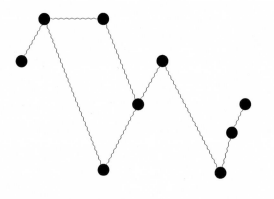

Full-on Falwell

Jimmy Swaggart skeevy

Jim Bakker creepy

Oral Roberts crazy

Joel Osteen innocuous

1990 1991 1992 1993 1994 1995 1996 1997 1998 1999 2000 2001 2002 2003 2004 2005 2006 2007 2008 2009 2010

1990: Has a television ministry

1992: Wants to quarantine AIDS patients over a decade into the crisis: "[I]t is the first time in the history of civilization in which the carriers of a genuine plague have not been isolated from the general population."

1997: "Abortion became OK because we decided it is OK. Where did we get the right to make that decision? Because we're our own god."

1997: Actually puts state money where his mouth is by starting ARKids First, which provides health care for low-income-household children.

2000: Says he didn't care about negative ads against him because God will ultimately judge.

2002: Says there should be no affirmative action for colleges, public employment, or state contracts.

2007: Is occasionally honorable: "[W]hat has made a huge mistake is that we've incarcerated so many of the people who really need drug rehab more than they need long-term incarceration."

2008: "When Katrina, a Cat-5 hurricane, hit the Gulf Coast, not one drop of oil was spilled off of those rigs out in the Gulf of Mexico. So we know that the technology to drill offshore is extraordinarily safe and environmentally friendly." Not only was Katrina a Category 4 when it hit, but many drops of oil spilled.

2009: Has a Fox "news" show, thus completing the circle back to 1990.

☞ **PREDICTION**

Well, he didn't give his kids a fetus to fondle, and it'd be a blast to watch him piss off Palin, and if he can keep the Jesus/"Queers are icky" shit to a minimum, he's probably the best non-Jeb choice the Republicans have. And, again, that's just sad.

---

see also

ANALYSES OF *other* **POSSIBLE REPUBLICAN PRESIDENTIAL CANDIDATES:**

Jim DeMint (pgs. 17-18), Mike Pence (pgs. 26-28), Jeb Bush (pgs. 30-31), Rick Santorum (pgs. 52-54), Sarah Palin (pgs. 74-75), Mitt Romney (pg. 78), Newt Gingrich (pgs. 104-105), Haley Barbour (pgs. 126-127), Tim Pawlenty (pgs. 128-129), Bobby Jindal (pgs. 169-171)

Three Poems

POEM ONE: *INSTANT*[1]

1. Legs

How's my favorite young stud doing?
You need a massage
Love to watch that
Those great legs running
Don't ruin my mental picture
You'll be way hot then

2. Touching

Did any girl give you a hand job this weekend?
So you're getting horny?
Did you spank it this weekend?
Wow
I am never too busy
Ha ha
Or tired. Helps me sleep
At your age seems like it would be daily
In the shower
In the bed
On your back
Love details
Kneeling

Completely naked
Cute butt bouncing in the air
Hmmmm
I always use lotion and the hand
Well, I have a totally stiff wood now
It must feel great spurting on the towel

3. Bulges

Is your little guy limp...or growing?
So you got a stiff one now?
I am as hard
As a rock
So tell me when
Yours reaches rock.
So a big bulge
Love to slip them off of you
And gram the one-eyed snake
Grab
Well, you're hard
And a little horny
Get a ruler and measure it for me
That's a great size
Take it out

4. Mom

Hope she didn't see anything.

1 From the transcripts of Republican Representative Mark Foley's messages to a teenage congressional page (obviously male). Foley resigned in 2006 over these and other messages and e-mails. Republican leadership had known about Foley's inappropriate (non-physical) contact with pages for at least a year. Edited for clarity because apparently Foley couldn't spell while typing with one hand.

POEM TWO *continues on the following page* >

POEM TWO: *ODE TO IMMORALITY*[2]

I am guilty of sexual immorality, and I take responsibility for the entire problem.

I am a deceiver and a liar.
There is a part of my life that is so
Repulsive and dark that I've been warring
Against it all of my adult life.

Different therapists have said different things
To me. My first therapist said, "You are
A heterosexual with homo-
Sexual attachments." And I wasn't
Sure what that meant. Now that we've processed this
Through, my current counselor says, "You're a
Heterosexual with complications."
And—and so I don't think the boxes work

For me. I think I have—I have some thoughts
In my life and some processes that just
Don't fit neatly into the boxes, which
I think is true for a lot of people.
The human race is such a mess. We have
Hatred and we have judgment and we have
Bitterness and we have high-mindedness
And arrogance and all types of sexual things.
We're all a mess. I'm a mess. I'm a disaster.

Jesus completed the work that he began in me,
Because I was praying about this the whole time.

2 From former minister Ted Haggard's "confession" to the congregation of the New Life Church on November 3, 2006, and an interview with Larry King on CNN on January 29, 2009. The evangelical Haggard was accused by a male prostitute of solicitation and smoking methamphetamine. Haggard was apparently a bottom. During the King interview, Haggard also confessed to masturbating in front of a young male church worker in a hotel room.

POEM THREE: *STALLING*[3]

All right, so let's start from the beginning. You went in the
bathroom. I could see your eyes. I saw you playing with your
fingers and then look up. Play with your fingers and then look
up. How long do you think you stood outside the stalls? And
when you went in the stalls, then what?
Did you do anything with your feet? Your foot did touch mine,
on my side of the stall. And then with the hand...I recall your
palm being up. When you pick up a piece of paper off the
ground, your palm would be down. What I saw was your fingers
come underneath the stall, you're actually touching the bottom
of the stall divider. I saw, I saw. I saw your left hand and I could
see the gold wedding ring when it went across. I could see that.
But I'm telling you that I could see that. Have you been successful in these bathrooms here before? I mean for any type of
other activities. It's embarrassing. I know you're not going to
fight me. But that's not the point. I would respect you and I still
respect you. I'm not trying to act like I have all kinds of power
or anything, but you're sitting here lying to a police officer. I
am trained in this and I know what I am doing. You put your
hand and rubbed it on the bottom of the stall. And I, I'm not
dumb, you can say I don't recall. I just, I just, I guess, I guess
I'm gonna say I'm just disappointed in you, sir. I just really am.
I expect this from the guy that we get out of the hood.

I mean, people vote for you.

Unbelievable, unbelievable.

I saw it with my own eyes.

Embarrassing, embarrassing.

3 From Republican Senator Larry Craig's interrogation by Sergeant Dave Karsnia in Minneapolis
on June 11, 2007. Craig was arrested at the
Minneapolis/St. Paul International Airport for suspi-
cion of lewd conduct for indicating to an undercover
officer that he desired a blumpkin by tapping his
foot while seated in a stall in the men's room.
Craig pleaded guilty and did not run for reelection
in 2008. All words are from Sergeant Karsnia.

No wonder why we're going down the tubes.

Shane called me up. "I've got two tickets to see Oliver North speak," he said. "They're free."

"Fuck that guy," I said, and as far as I was concerned, that was that.

A day or so later, Shane said, "C'mon, it'll be fun." He had puppy dog eyes and a hell of a pout. There was no resisting. But when I >

agreed, Shane said, "Okay, but you gotta promise me you're not going to make a scene." He had gotten the tickets from his boss, and he didn't want to lose his job if I threw blood on the good colonel. I said I'd be good. Shane's dewy brown eyes told me that he didn't believe me.

When we arrived at the Cajundome (no, really), we saw a line of protesters, carrying signs, chanting against North. The picket line contained at least two of our professors and several good friends. I understand why they yelled at me for heading into the big auditorium to see a criminal transformed into some kind of bizarro outlaw Superman in a military uniform tell us all what was what with Central America, a place he had no small part of turning to shit back in the 1980s. I said to my friends, "Free speech, man, it ain't pretty. But it's all we got." So I went in and listened to him bob and weave and justify and pontificate. At the end, an obviously planted man got to the microphone and said, in a halting Spanish accent, that he was a Nicaraguan who was grateful for North breaking the law to arm the contras. I was so done. And when he finished, everyone stood up to applaud, except me. I don't remember if Shane stood. No one said I had to be polite. But I didn't scream, "War criminal." I didn't tell everyone around me that they were tools of empire.

No, I just sat there without standing, without clapping, and the voices started around me, "Hey, why isn't he clapping?" And then someone asked me, "Why aren't you clapping? That's an American hero." I just said that I was there to listen. "You should be clapping."

"Sorry. I can't." My inability to clap for criminals has really stymied my ability to make friends.

And when we left, Shane complimented me on my good behavior. I thanked him for the tickets. Then I went home and bathed with a steel brush as if I had just been exposed to nuclear radiation. ℞Ⓟ

IT WAS THE FOURTH OF JULY IN RED STATE AMERICA, 2009. Louisiana, to be precise. I had celebrated in the way of the locals, by eating various kinds of grilled meat, and yet I still felt empty inside, like I needed to be among people who knew the >

meaning, the true meaning of the date when our forefathers declared their independence with a Declaration of Independence. So I read about the local Tea Party going on in a local park, even though it was hotter than Satan's taint outside. After asking if any of the other carnivores wanted to go with me, and being abandoned by all those who wished to remain in ignorance, alone I headed out.

In the park, there were about a hundred or so people gathered in the three strips of shade provided by the trees. I walked through, looking at signs that proclaimed the people present disapproved of socialism, liberalism, and Barack Obama. One gentleman's sign expressed his desire to not be anally raped. "I will not grab my ankles," it read, although, considering his gut, which made him seem as if he was pregnant with a toddler, he seemed a bit ambitious about how low he could bend.

I walked by a man holding a sign with an image from the end of the film *Planet of the Apes*, with Charlton Heston on his knees before a ruined Statue of Liberty. President Obama's face was photoshopped into one of the apes. I asked the man who was carrying it if he had gotten it off the Internet. "No," the man said, "I made it myself." He was going to post it, though, so that others might use his work. He expected no royalties.

Then I bumped into another man, garbed from hat to boots in Revolutionary War soldier clothes.

Actual conversation:

ME: Did you make that yourself?
MAN IN COLONIAL DRAG: No, Betsy Ross made it.
ME: (pause) So... um... General Washington?
MAN: No, but I'm proud to be one of his aides.
ME: (thinking about an AIDS joke, but wanting to survive the day)
Well, Ms. Ross did a fine job. Can I take your picture?
(Man smiles. I take the picture.)

The man would later lead the crowd in the Pledge of Allegiance, in front of a band's drum kit that had a Confederate flag dangling from it. A woman in costume would sing the National Anthem. Another man would read from the Bible. It was really a catch-all kind of event.

Inside the air-conditioned rec center gym, another 200 people gathered to watch a John Birch Society video about how communists are taking over the country. Some long-haired man in what looked like a cut-rate Jack Sparrow buccaneer's coat told us at the end that the event was not sponsored by the John Birch Society, but that he just thought the video was informative. And he was right. I had no idea how minor adjustments to taxes on the wealthiest Americans was actually something Marx had predicted. Or Nostradamus. The beards get confusing.

There were tables with all kinds of information about health care, abortion, taxes. I heard one table attendant hold forth on how fascism was more widespread than communism, but that we need to be cautious about both. It didn't make sense then. It doesn't make sense now. But the people he spoke to were nodding. It made sense to them. That was actually more frightening because it meant that they were just making up new definitions to the words, or, more likely, simply conflating them to mean "bad."

Much like a sign there, which read, "46 million without health insurance... who are they kidding? 9.7 million are not even Americans." How do you argue with someone who thinks having sick illegal immigrants working all over the country is not a bad thing?

No, instead you sigh, thinking that it's too hot a day. You debate in your mind whether or not this is a real movement or just a bunch of people who too readily believe all the goddamn lies they're fed. You get a free sno-cone (sour apple flavor). You listen to the costumed kids sing, "God Bless America." You leave when the Confederate-flagged band starts to cover Lee Greenwood's fucking song. You go to see fireworks downtown after the local symphony plays. You hear that people around here don't put pro-choice or pro-Obama stickers on their cars because they'll get keyed. You know this is America, too, yes, here in the Red States, where your family lives, and, unlike the Tea Party–goers, you recognize it because, even as they celebrate a so-called "revolution" and hope for another, some things never change. **RP**

THE TEA PARTY:
HOWARD DEAN'S SLOPPY SECONDS

YOU EVER WONDER WHERE THE HELL THE TEA PARTY CAME FROM, with its cry of "I want my country back"? Hey, lookie here: It's former Vermont Governor Howard Dean, whose online organization that led to his presidential run was called "Take Back America." >

1. And, look, Dean posters and bumper stickers proclaimed, "I want my country back!"

2. In a 2003 speech, Dean said, "This is a movement for every American to take their country back from special interests."

3. A July 2005 *Washington Post* article said, "When he is exercised by a crowd, the flush creeps up his neck, and he turns into the guy who stood on podiums during his failed bid for the 2004 Democratic presidential nomination and roared, 'I want my country back!'"

4. At the 2004 Democratic National Convention, Dean said, "Together we can take our country back, and only you have the power to make it happen." That man was ahead of his time, he was.

Now, this is not to say that Deaniacs, as the good doctor's supporters were called, just became Obamaniacs and then became genuinely insane by joining the Tea Party. However, the Howard Dean[1] movement was based on anger at the Bush administration, and Dean got pounded by the press for it, just because he yelled excitedly at a loud political rally and because his campaign was a truly grassroots action, which scared the hell out of the establishment. Obama was able to channel the Dean-fluffed rage into another kind of rebellious energy four years after Dean, but, ultimately, that uncashed check of Bush hatred had to be brought to the bank. The Tea Party and their teabagging ways are residual Bush resentment with a healthy dose of good old-fashioned racism and stupidity.[2]

So when Glenn Beck asked, in June 2007, "Do you ever see a time coming in this country, if Congress and the White House doesn't get their act together, that people stand up and say, 'I want my country back'?" he didn't even realize that he was just stepping into the bed after Howard Dean had already had his turn. RP

---

1 I have a great deal of downright admiration for Dean. He's inspiring, smart, and curses like a drunken Quentin Tarantino character in private.
2 Other "I want my country back" campaigns: Dick Gephardt in 1998, Bill Clinton and Ross Perot in 1992, and, with total racist intent, Pat Buchanan in 1996.

**THREE OBAMA URBAN LEGENDS /
CONSPIRACY THEORIES THAT CAME FROM
SATIRICAL BLOGS (AND THE LINES THAT
DEMONSTRATE THEY'RE SATIRE)**

LET'S GO BEYOND THE MAINSTREAM INSANITY OF BARACK OBAMA'S CITIZENSHIP and head deep into your Gmail inbox, where you keep finding spam forwarded to you by your cousin >

Jesse, the one that Aunt Henrietta and Uncle Deke keep locked in a basement where his only friends are his fellow Free Republic commenters, Glenn Beck, and the cockroaches. Yeah, your cousin's a freakin' retard because he doesn't even know what's a joke and what's real. Why? Because retards will believe anything.[1]

1. Obama apologized for the Declaration of Independence. (from the conservative blog IMAO, July 3, 2009)

Obvious satire: "Queen Elizabeth the Second said that she would 'consider' accepting the apology if Obama would 'take back this stupid iPod and send me a Kindle 2.'"

Why is this obvious satire? Queen Elizabeth II loves her iPod and walks around Buckingham Palace in a daze with her ear buds firmly pressed into her royal ear holes.

2. The KKK endorsed Obama for president. (from the British blog The Daily Squib, February 7, 2008)

Obvious satire: Grand Turk Cletus Monroe opines, "Hell, I'll even adopt a black kid from Africa before I vote for Hillary."

Why is this obvious satire? Because Hillary Clinton is a well-known Klan member.

This one got so popular that the actual Ku Klux Klan issued an actual statement, with national director Thomas Robb asking rhetorically (and incoherently), "Is he willing to stand for the protection of white men, women and children who are quickly to be America's new minority"? (That question mark is outside the quotation marks because Robb used a period.)

3. Obama will issue an executive order banning anyone over sixty from owning a gun. (from the conservative blog Jumping in Pools, January 27, 2009)

1 Regarding the word "retard," many actually mentally disabled people would be able to tell the difference between reality and satire. However, one is a "retard" if one truly believes that Glenn Beck is smart.

Obvious satire: An "unnamed aide" to a deputy attorney general designate says, "President Obama comes from a new sort of politics, where divisive issues like firearms do not apply to him."

Why is this obvious satire? Probably because it says "this is SATIRE" just above the article.

It was not, however, enough of a label for National Rifle Association members, who flooded the organization's office with questions and outraged comments, so much so that the NRA issued a statement that denied the rumor and educated concerned old fucks with guns that "it's worth mentioning that these [executive] orders and memoranda aren't secret." A link to the White House was provided. 🅿

Founding Fathers Fun Time

Sarah Palin, on Fox "news"' *On the Record*, April 23, 2010:

> "A state governor has got to make sure that they are remembering who they are serving. It's the people who hired them, their state's voters, and they do what's best for the people who did hire them. Sometimes that is in conflict with the federal government."

George Washington, in a 1783 letter to the Marquis de Lafayette, on the need for a Constitution:

> "[T]he probability, at least I fear it is, [is] that local, or state Politics will interfere too much with that more liberal and extensive plan of government which wisdom and foresight, freed from the mist of prejudice, would dictate ... the honor, power, and true Interest of this Country must be measured by a Continental scale; and that every departure therefrom weakens the Union, and may ultimately break the band, which holds us together."

GREAT MOMENTS IN WEALTH REDISTRIBUTION #2

In November 2007, when she was the still-popular governor of Alaska, Palin proposed a 10 percent increase on net oil profits because the state needed more revenue. She raised the tax rate from 22.5 percent to 25 percent. Palin wanted an additional 10 percent minimum tax on production, but the legislature would not go along. She called the legislature back into a special session in order to address the fact that the Petroleum Profits Tax was not generating enough money for the state's budget. BP made noise that it was rethinking its operations in Alaska, but decided the hundreds of thousands of barrels of oil it was pumping were more important than a stand on the socialist activities of the Republican governor.

FORMER ALASKA GOVERNOR & VICE PRESIDENTIAL CANDIDATE

Sarah Palin

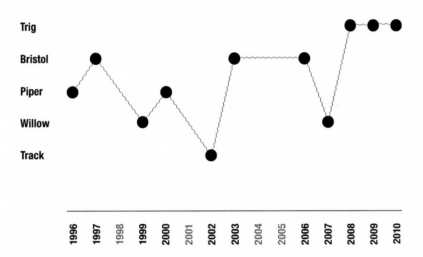

1996: When she was still in the fishing industry (and on the Wasilla City Council), she went to the Anchorage J.C. Penney's to see Ivana Trump. " 'We want to see Ivana,' said Palin, who admittedly smells like salmon for a large part of the summer,[1] 'because we are so desperate in Alaska for any semblance of glamour and culture.'"[2] This proves to be the greatest indicator of her future desires.

1997: Once she became mayor of Wasilla, she fired a bunch of public servants, including the police chief and town librarian because "Palin asked her three times in her first weeks in office whether she would agree to remove controversial books. The librarian said she would not." There was actually an uproar that forced Palin to put her back in the position.

1999: As mayor, she presided over the wedding of two Walmart employees at Walmart. "It was so sweet," said Palin, who fought back tears during the nuptials. "It was so Wasilla."

2000: Worked to secure tons of federal earmarks for her town, including millions of dollars for a rail project. This was just the start of the earmark gravy train she made sure stopped regularly in Alaska.

2002: Ran for lieutenant governor. Lost.

2003: Appointed chair of the Alaska Oil and Gas Conservation Commission. Quit after less than a year.

2006: Ran for governor. Among things she said: no abortion in cases of rape and incest; senior citizens "are my delight"; guns are awesome; and more oil drilling. Won.

2007: Issued a press release affirming the right of Alaskans to hunt from helicopters. Wait... not "hunting": It's a "predator-management system."

2008: Oh, you know. John McCain secured his place in political hell.

2009: Quit as governor, saying, honestly, everyone would be better off if she was gone.

2010: Got a job at Fox "news." Wrote on her hand. Threatens to run for president. Made a terrible TV show on TLC. Forced Bristol to dance.

Analysis continues >

---

1 I will claim remarkable restraint in not making a joke at this observation.
2 However, this description led poor, punchy researcher Kristina to name Palin "Salmon Snatch," and added "as a woman, I do feel slightly bad for making that up." But only slightly.

ANALYSIS OF POSSIBLE REPUBLICAN PRESIDENTIAL CANDIDATES (#6 *of* 11)

FORMER ALASKA GOVERNOR &
VICE PRESIDENTIAL CANDIDATE

Sarah Palin

continued

☞**PREDICTION**

She has to run for president, if for no other reason than to keep Jethro and Ellie Mae in shoes with soles. Look, she's in this for cash money and a TV deal. The second she's out of the race, she cashes in on how mean the meanies were to her. If she doesn't run, then she's revealed as the fraud she actually is. She's Lady Macbeth crossed with Imelda Marcos with a sauce made of Leona Helmsley. If she somehow stumbles into the nomination, she'll bail.

FORMER SOMETHING OR OTHER

Mitt Romney

NOTE:

Mitt Romney is a boring asshole who has flipped on so many things he believes that, while he may use his millions to buy himself a little time in the primaries, no one beyond creepy-ass fellow Mormons are gonna vote for his skeevy, hypocritical ass. Gay rights, health care, taxes. Just about anything he could change positions on, he did like a high-priced hooker in a ménage with two old men and a night's worth of Viagra. So fuck him for wasting everyone's time: no chart, nothing. It ain't even worth mocking at this point. Seriously, someone just show the rabbits to this deluded egomaniac's pitiful end of what might have been an honorable political career.

Oh, and Ron Paul? No.

Part 4:

THE EQUINOX

"I" RIDING ON AN AIRPLANE WITH SOMEONE WHO TALKS TO GOD

I WAS IN THE AISLE SEAT on the Continental flight from San Francisco to Houston, half-heartedly flirting with the young woman who had the window. Then a woman who looked to be in her mid-fifties with bright orange hair and a deep hick accent took the middle, which I took as my cue to read. The >

older woman started talking to the young woman, and I was half-heartedly eavesdropping while waiting for us to take off when I heard the older woman say, "Well, then God told me that I was going to get better." The young woman nodded politely and she went back to staring out the window. I sat for a while, wondering if I should engage, wondering if I felt like hearing a story of someone miraculously getting better and thanking Lord Jeeezus for it. Then again, I was bored.

"Excuse me," I said, "I'm sorry, but I couldn't help overhearing: You said God spoke to you? Do you mean he healed you?"

"Oh, no," she said, "God told me what I needed to do to get better."

"And when you say God talked to you..."

"I don't mean that a man in a long white beard and robes appeared to me." And then she told me her story. She had worked for Exxon in south Texas for years, hardly ever sick at all, and then one day she got violently ill. She couldn't eat, couldn't hold anything down. She was in a hospital for months on end. The doctors did every kind of test they could think of, and nothing was coming up. One doctor even suggested that the whole thing was in her head, which was fine, but didn't make her able to take in solid food. Finally, someone diagnosed her with an extremely rare digestive condition, and she could only be fed with a tube directly into her stomach. She lived like this for a couple of years, taking tons of medication, occasionally needing to be rushed to the hospital by her husband, wasting away and never able to do anything but go from home to doctor and back. Then one night she had a dream, as clear and beautiful a dream as she had ever had. In it, she saw a blue sky and clouds; a male voice from on high told her that she needed to put herself in his hands and trust that he would take care of her. The next day, she told her husband to throw out every medication that she had been taking, to just put it in a trash bag and bring it out to the garbage cans. Her husband argued but eventually gave in. She contacted her doctor and said that she had done so. The doctor was furious and told her she would suffer mightily from withdrawal from some of the painkillers. As you can imagine, since this is the story of a miracle, the doctor was wrong. A few weeks later she had the same dream. But the voice this time told her that she needed to get the tube taken out of her, that it was infected, that it was time for her to start eating again. She went to her doctor, who refused at first to pull out the feeding tube, but said that since she hadn't had any withdrawal symptoms from the medications, he would do it. When he pulled out the tube, what do you think he saw? Of course, she had an infection. He treated it, but she went home that day without the means to eat. She told her husband that God would give her a sign. She was watching TV the next day and she saw a commercial, with a blue sky, with clouds, and a voice telling about how delicious peaches were. She knew, right then and there, and she sent her husband to the store to buy a single peach. He returned with it, and, for the first time in five years, she bit into a piece of food.

She mimed this for me, the act of biting that peach, and she said that the juice hit her flavor-deprived tongue and exploded across her taste buds. "I had never eaten anything better," she said. It took her a couple of hours to eat the peach because her jaw muscles had atrophied from lack of use. Slowly, she built up to where she could eat most things. Her doctor called it a miracle. Her husband was Greek Orthodox, and she started attending his church. There, she is known as the woman who can talk directly to God. People ask her to pray for different things in their lives, and, since she believes she does have a red phone to the Lord, she picks and chooses what she does ask God for.

Her husband was just north of San Francisco, prepping a boat. After taking care of her nonstop for years, she had said they would do whatever he wanted. He wanted the two of them to take a months-long cruise down the California coast, down Mexico, through the Panama Canal, and then up the Gulf of Mexico back to their home in Texas. She was flying back to get things ready.

What went through my head was, "Well, of course, that early doctor was right: you're crazy and obviously your illness was a result of your madness." She wasn't proselytizing, she wasn't converting; no, she was telling a story I had asked about. Wow, I thought, another Texas matron who believes in magic and miracles and invisible sky wizards swooping in and entering one's dreams. Good to always have it reconfirmed that such faith is real.

She asked about my religion, and I said that I'm an atheist. "See?" she offered. "We can get along just fine."

I asked her where was the Exxon office where she worked. She looked at me confusedly. "Oh, I didn't work in an office. I couldn't do that." I must have looked confused back. "I worked on the drilling rigs out in the fields in Texas. I did it for nearly thirty years. I'd wildcat, I'd climb up on the rigs, I did it all. I loved it. I only stopped because I got sick."

I did some quick math in my head, putting her starting work drilling for oil in Texas in the late 1970s. I was stunned. "Wait, you were, like, on the derricks and pumps?"

"That's right. I'd build them. I'd repair them. I worked outside the whole time."

"In the '70s, right? You must have been one of the first women to be out on the rigs."

"I was in the first group of women ever hired to do it."

All of a sudden, she became a hell of a lot more interesting to me than as a miracle survivor of a disease that could not be named. She was a pioneer.

Then she opened up about the rest of her life. She grew up in southern Ohio and wanted to follow her father and brother into the steel industry, but the companies wouldn't let women out of the secretarial pool. So, at seventeen, being independent and having a wild streak, she hitchhiked her way down to Texas, where she heard that the oil companies might be opening up to hire women. She was one of five women hired just west of Houston, so, on her shifts, often she was the only woman. She was hazed endlessly, and she learned that she had to be the meanest person there: "I learned to cuss worse than any of the boys would. That showed 'em."

"You're like this feminist hero," I said.

"No, I'm not a feminist."

"What are you talking about? You were one of the first women to break a wall in an industry that's still dominated by men. Did you fight for your job?"

"Until I became the old girl that everyone knew not to mess with, sure."

"Then you fought for women's rights."

For a moment, she thought about my filtering of her life through this historical prism. Or maybe she was just thinking that I was the crazy guy on the seat next to her. Either way, she said, "If you want to call it that, then sure. But I just wanted to do the work."

I leaned over and the young woman at the window sat staring out, ear buds tuning us out. I wanted to tell her about what the woman in the middle seat had done, how every little victory on the road to equality made it easier on everyone who came later. But she probably wouldn't have cared. ▶P

I WAS RAISED A POOR WHITE BIGOT. My Jewish grandmother scoffed at "the schwartzes." My brother would drive through black neighborhoods in Lafayette and, bizarrely, shake a plastic devil's pitchfork at families on their porches. My Italian father thought we should nuke Iran during the hostage crisis, that we >

should have nuked Vietnam, and that capital punishment should be broadcast on ABC's *Wide World of Sports*. For him, the worst of all were gay men—just pedophiles waiting to strike. He was worried sick that his bookish, theater-loving son was gonna be some craven sword swallower or something.

So I went away to college, Tulane University, rock solid in my hawkish, Reagan-worshipping, gay-fearful Neanderthal retardation. And, beyond the immersion in cultures and races outside of my narrow purview, I took a course in political philosophy with Professor Jean Danielson. We read Hobbes and Locke, and I began to think that maybe the world didn't need to be this brutish place, filled with isolated people who condemned others for their existence. By the time we got to Rousseau and by the time I was going to the Desire housing project with a friend to have dinners at his aunt's apartment and by the time I was going to see REM and Frank Zappa in concert, I was in one of those full-blown existential crises that you get to go through if you pay attention at school.

Oh, and I was a member of the College Republicans. And it was 1984, and Ronald Reagan was going to win reelection. We'd sit around in each other's rooms and laugh at how Reagan seemed like he was kicking Walter Mondale's ass in debates. Between, you know, snorts of cocaine and sex with the pure conservative girls who lived on the floor below.

I was walking across campus with a dorm friend from Boston, heading to a November meeting of the College Republicans. He said to me, in a voice resonant with Thurston Howell III intonations, "I can't believe the Democrats want to stop the president from building more nuclear missiles. We have to keep up with the Soviets, don't you think?"

In one of those rare, startling moments of complete clarity, I stopped in my tracks and slowly said, "No. No, I think we have enough nukes." Thurston stared at me, quizzically, perhaps waiting for the punch line. I continued, "I don't think I can go to this meeting." I turned around, headed back over to see a Democratic girl, Mary, at my dorm, quit the College Republicans, and joined the newspaper to do investigative reporting. Luckily, I was only seventeen, so I couldn't vote. I would have voted for Reagan, and that's even more karma I'd've been working off for a long, long time. ꝑ

THE SOURCE OF ALL EVIL: KARL ROVE

THERE'S ALL KINDS OF MOTHERFUCKERS IN THIS WORLD. There's power-grabbing motherfuckers like Dick Cheney, manipulating facts and circumstance for the assertion of an ideology. There's greedy mother-fuckers like your Bernie Madoffs or your Lloyd >

Blankfeins. And then there's a special category: motherfuckers who just like fucking mothers. They will fuck your mother just for the delight of coming up to you when they're done, telling you to smell their fingers, and laughing when they inform you that you're smelling your own mom's pussy. Karl Rove is one of those motherfuckers, a man who raised fucking mothers to an art form, like a Picasso of spin, like a Rodin of the attack ad.

His life is a rewrite of the Rolling Stones' "Sympathy for the Devil" set in the filthy world of American political consultancy, in which he ran a firm for nearly twenty years. You could try to list every terrible deed Rove has committed, from spending his college years in the early 1970s teaching young Republicans seminars in Nixonian dirty tricks to the 1986 Texas gubernatorial campaign, when Rove, who was working for the insane Republican Bill Clements, bugged his own office and blamed the Democratic candidate to the 1990 Texas agriculture commissioner campaign where he used the FBI to help destroy the reputation of Democrat Jim Hightower in order to get Republican Rick Perry elected. You could move on to when he sent goons in cheap suits down to Florida in 2000 to stop the Bush/Gore recount. You could try to talk about his role in outing undercover CIA agent Valerie Plame in 2003 as punishment for her husband, Joseph Wilson, breaking the administration's omertà over the lies that got us into the Iraq War. Pleased to meet you. Hope you guess my name.

So, instead, let's focus on two things: Rove's use of American homophobia to tarnish candidates and his fearless destruction of soldiers who fought in Vietnam.

Through the campaigns he ran for George W. Bush, Karl Rove led one of the most sustained assaults on gays and lesbians in America. When Bush was running against Democratic Governor Ann Richards in Texas in 1994, Rove started a whisper campaign that the older, unmarried Richards was a lesbian. And, since Richards had given a couple of state government positions to openly gay Texans, Rove got state senator and Bush campaign coordinator Ben Ratliff to say she was "appointing avowed homosexual activists." Of course it worked. In Texas, in 1994, how could a queer-loving, presumed lesbian continue to be governor? Who cares if she was actually good at the job if homosexuals might be getting all homosexual around Austin?

Rove repeated this tactic in the 2000 presidential campaign. After Senator John McCain won the New Hampshire primary over Bush, Rove went after McCain with a breathtaking savagery in the next primary state, South Carolina,

throwing every possible allegation at McCain, including that he had fathered a mixed-race child with a black prostitute. Because McCain had spoken to the Log Cabin Republicans, also known to the GOP as "those gay conservatives we're gonna ignore," Rove orchestrated phone calls to South Carolina Republicans calling McCain "the fag candidate." This shit ain't even subtle.

In 2004, Rove helped to make sure that anti-gay marriage initiatives were put on the ballots in eleven states, including Ohio, in order to assure that the evangelical GOP base would turn out in order to vote their hatred and, by the way, vote for the reelection of George W. Bush. In all three races, Rove demonstrated that homophobia is to the United States what cheese is to France. He studied and exploited the prejudices and idiocies of Americans like an evil sociologist.

You almost have to admire, though, the way that Rove took down three former soldiers wounded in battle by making them seem insane or traitorous. While the fact that you might have run through the jungle, shooting a gun and avoiding getting killed, doesn't necessarily make you qualified to be an elected official, one's actions during war do say something about one's basic human character. You'd think that if you survived torture in a North Vietnamese POW camp or were blown up at Khe Sanh or saved the crew of your boat in a battle on the Duong Keo river, you might have proven your patriotism. Not to Rove. Indeed, for Rove, your military service is nothing to be honored; it is merely rhetorical cannon fodder.

Take John McCain. As part of that cruel South Carolina primary, Rove started another whisper campaign, this time saying that McCain's five years in captivity left him mentally unstable. Take Senator Max Cleland. In 2002, Cleland wanted the employees of the proposed Department of Homeland Security to have the same union protections civil servants in other departments had. During the 2002 midterm elections, Rove put out an ad equating Cleland, who lost three limbs from a grenade in Vietnam, with Saddam Hussein and Osama bin Laden. Take John Kerry. During Bush's 2004 reelection campaign, Rove coordinated with the Swift Boat Veterans for Truth, calling into question every aspect of Kerry's multiple-decorated service in the Vietnam War. All three men lost. Does it need to be said that Rove never served in the military? Does it need to be repeated that George W. Bush didn't even fulfill his Texas Air National Guard Service? Or that Cleland's opponent, Saxby Chambliss, received five draft deferments due to a football injury? Karl Rove has done more to spit on Vietnam veterans than every hippie combined, yet conservatives love him.

The truly awful thing is that even this doesn't scratch the surface. It doesn't get into how he used his positions in the Bush administration to merge politics and policy. Anything Bush did was simply to appeal to the basest instincts of voters or to shore up his own power. In his role in the shadows, Rove made the terrorist attacks of September 11, 2001, into a Republican-owned political issue while making opposing the president on anything akin to treason. What else? Christ, we could go with the US Attorneys he had fired for not investigating Democrats or the people who have gone to jail because of Rove's vendettas. Yet Bush paid no political cost. Rove made sure of that. Rove has revealed, and he revels in, how easy it is to yank the collars of Americans and of the American media.

Frighteningly, Rove seems like he enjoys this. He sees the whole electoral process as a game, and, for a long period of time, he was its grand champion. He smiles at the adversity. He jokes with reporters. He danced on stage at the White House Correspondents' Dinner. Some serial killers are in awful pain when they commit their crimes. Some, though, get off on it. Rove is the Ed Gein of political animals. His high school yearbook says that Rove was "a never stop to ponder kind of guy." That means he never thinks about the consequences. There is only action to an end. Every campaign is war, every opponent the enemy. And, even if he is very wrong, he says that he's always right.

Watch him on Fox "news." He is on regularly as a commentator now that he is out of office and he no longer runs a consulting firm. Watch and see his wheels turning, ever plotting, offering hints of what he might do if he were in the game. He has said he is not going to run another campaign. But his dream was to create a permanent Republican majority. He is returning now, filling his baggy pockets with Wall Street cash to fund his wars. Like a swarm of seven-year locusts or Godzilla gone back to sea, he is only waiting for the right season to wreak destruction once more. The Mayan calendar says it'll be in 2012.

When Lee Atwater, a fellow dirty trickster and close friend of Karl Rove, one of the gurus of Reagan's and then Bush I's campaigns, the man who perfected the attack mode of campaigning, including the racist Willie Horton ad, was dying of brain cancer in 1991, he had an epiphany about the world he helped to create. He called the unmitigated greed of the Reagan/Bush era a "spiritual vacuum at the heart of American society, this tumor of the soul." It was an attempt at deathbed redemption. Rove will have no such Kurtzian moment of realizing the horror. He is a man who took a look at the American body politic, already handcuffed to a bed, and decided to take a shit on it and set the room on fire. ℞

Part 5:

THE FALL OF THE MEDIA

THE CASE OF THE COMPROMISED COED

"CAN I TALK TO YOU?"

said one of the resident advisers in my dorm, Sharp Hall, at Tulane University, as he sashayed into my room. "You work for the paper, right?" Me, I was just some punk freshman movie critic for the *Hullabaloo*, the student rag, loaded with fancy words and the ability to describe John >

Malkovich's acting with a clever metaphor involving weasels. All of a sudden, here was this handsome older man, a senior, muscular, curly-haired. I wondered if he was coming on to me. I wondered if I was ready to explore. "Yes, I do," I answered, expectantly.

"I need to talk to you. But it's got to be off-the-record. Can I just be an anonymous source?" His eyes were dreamy, his mustache well-combed. *You can tell me anything you like, Sailor*, I wanted to say, but instead, confused, I told him I'd protect his identity. "Good, because I could lose my job. A football player assaulted three women in the showers here, and nothing's going to happen to the guy."

I paused before speaking. If I had been a smarter teenager, I would have told him where to stick his scoop, smacked him on his ass, and told him to forget about it and let's go to his large RA room to work it all out. Or I would have said that I was just a wannabe Ebert with no ambition beyond being able to use my thumb on TV to indicate my pleasure or displeasure with flicks.

But I had just recently undergone a conversion, from apathetically conservative to righteously liberal, and I was ready to prove my new street cred. I told the RA, with gam muscles so hard they could crush walnuts and shorts so tight that his balls looked like a dead guinea pig attached to his thigh, that I'd take the case.

I went to my editor and made him swear on a dog-eared copy of *All the President's Men* that I could have the story if I told him what it was. He agreed, but when I said what was going on, he asked, "You think you have the chops, Papa?"

"I have the chops. And the T-bone."

"Then get your trenchcoat and notepad, you son of a bitch, and nail this fucker."

I discovered, upon interviewing the women involved, that, thankfully, the perp wasn't a starter. A red-shirted player for the Green Wave had somehow made his way past the security desk to the floor of Sharp Hall where the females lived. The player, described as a large, black male, which, at Tulane in 1984, would have made him stick out like a burnt Rice Krispie, had staked out the showers. When one of the females, call her Rhonda, went into a stall, he walked into it with her and pressed against her. Rhonda screamed, and the perp, call him Dwight, ran. He grabbed the towel off another student and grabbed the ass of a third on his way out. Sounded like someone didn't realize that *Porky's* was a fictional movie and women didn't actually think it was innocuous child's play to eyeball them and attempt to rape them in the showers. The football player had been brought in and faced expulsion, but he had been cleared with a slap on the wrist by the time his hearing was over. I promised Rhonda and the other two that I would make sure that justice was done.

I talked to some of the people in charge, the campus cops, a representative of the president, and none would comment on the case. All they would tell me was that there had been "egregious" errors in the investigation and hearing. Back at the *Hullabaloo*, we laughed like dingoes next to a dying kangaroo at how ludicrous it was to use that word. Hell, we didn't even know what it meant. My editor looked it up in the dictionary. "Flagrant." Huh. You learn something new every day. Guess that's what college is for.

Yeah, it was all fun and games. Me against the man. I was riding that journalistic power trip like it was a twenty-buck-a-blow whore and I just got off the battleship on shore leave with a pocket full of cash and a hard-on, fluffed by my editor, who massaged my shoulders when I sat in the newsroom typing. I wrote the article and included a long list of the officials, from the student government president to the dean, from the bottom to the top, who refused to talk to me. We went to press and waited for the explosions.

And then I started to get phone calls in my dorm room. And the game ended. And it became real.

The first one was from one of the victims, the one who had been groped. Even though I hadn't mentioned any of their names, she cried when she said she wished she hadn't said anything. She wanted to just finish her semester in peace, and she said she wouldn't talk to me anymore about the case. The next was from Rhonda's mother. She yelled at me and threatened to sue me if I made her daughter appear in any way other than as an innocent victim. I assured her that I had no intention of doing anything else. Then Rhonda's father got on the phone and said he'd kick my ass if I said anything negative about his daughter. I had nothing negative to say, and I told him as much. The third call was from the office of Tulane University President Eamon Kelly. It was his secretary.

"President Kelly would like to meet with you."

I looked at an unfinished English lit paper in my typewriter. "I can possibly do it tomorrow. Would that work for you?"

"No," she said, "you don't understand. He wants to meet with you right now."

"I have to finish this—"

"We'll see you in a few minutes."

The first thought that crossed my mind was that my scholarship was fucked. As I walked across campus, crossing Freret Street, making my way past the academic buildings to the main administrative manse on St. Charles, it dawned on me that getting called to the president's office was not the same as getting called to the principal's office. I realized that a paddling was not a possibility, which was good, but it meant I had no idea what was about to happen. I was slightly sickened, and then I told myself to get arrogant. I'm the goddamn press. I'm an honor student, a National Merit Finalist. Yeah, motherfuckers, I was righteous. Besides, I had been to President Kelly's house for a reception earlier in the year. We had said hello and shaken hands. We were practically friends.

I walked to the receiving room, and the secretary immediately sent me in. Kelly's enormous wood-paneled, green-rugged office held a long table and shelves, loaded with what seemed to be law books, as well as his impossibly huge desk. Kelly shook my hand. "Lee, right?" I nodded and immediately asked what he wanted to see me about. He gestured to me to sit down on one of the tall, green padded chairs at the endless table. "I invited you here because I wanted to talk about the Dwight case."

"I kind of thought so."

He sat across from me and picked up a copy of my article from the table. I wanted to call him out, to say that this was intimidation, even if doing so made me vomit on the truly lovely wood floors. He read the paragraph of no-commenters and said, "All of these people wanted to talk to you. But they couldn't."

"I would have been fair to them."

"That's not the issue. They simply couldn't. Legally. Some of them wanted very badly to speak."

I was confused. How could someone be denied their right to speak? "I'm sorry, but I don't get it. Dwight did something wrong. It looks like he got off because he was a football player."

Kelly, balding head gleaming in the sunlight through the large windows that overlooked the moss-draped trees of the Garden District, paused. Then he said, "What do you know about due process?" I didn't answer because it was a phrase I'd heard but didn't fully get.[1] I didn't want to seem stupid or say that everything I knew about it came from *Miami Vice* and *The French Connection*.

1 Believe it or not, there was a time when *Law and Order* wasn't on twenty-four hours a day.

"Due process exists to protect the rights of someone accused of a crime. It's the rules you're supposed to follow." I knew that crooks got off because cops forgot to read Miranda rights, sure. "What happened in this case is that we wanted to expel the student. But he had certain rights, even here at school. Our attorney said that he had been denied those rights and that egregious errors had occurred in the process. Because of that, we had to close the case." He spoke to me slowly, treating me like an idiot, which, in this realm, I kind of was.

"Why egregious?" I asked, as if the existence of that word somehow offended me. Kelly didn't answer. Of course. It was lawyer-speak as a way of not admitting a conspiracy, a kind of Nixonian shrug, that mistakes were just made and no one could be held responsible and therefore sued directly. "What were the mistakes?"

"I can't reveal that either." Because local law enforcement hadn't gotten involved, they could keep everything private. The fix was in. And a freshman at the student paper was not going to un-fix it.

I looked around the room, wondering, I suppose, if this was some kind of joke, and back at Kelly. "Why did you bring me here?" I asked.

He gestured at a folder, thick with all kinds of papers, that was also on the table. "That's all the work we did on this case. I brought you here to talk to you face to face because this is a very serious matter. You need to know that we wanted to do something about Dwight. But we couldn't."

"So he gets away with it."

"That's not how I would put it," he told me. And the meeting was done.

I left and walked back across campus, heading to the *Hullabaloo* office. I was furious about the whole situation. I kicked benches and tossed trash cans around because what Kelly said had made perverse sense, and yet that meant the guy was going to be back on campus, maybe even in classes with Rhonda, maybe becoming a starting player on the football team, cheered and worshipped.

My editor was pissed off, saying that Kelly had been trying to silence me. He stood there while I wrote a follow-up article. He was right, you know. Now, I see that I had stirred up something, that other people involved probably wanted to break ranks and talk, that Kelly was doing everything he could to protect the school from lawsuit.

And then, as my beliefs evolved over the next few years, I understood, too, that Kelly was also right about the errors, that if you believe in due process, you have to abide it. And if the people in charge fuck it up, if they don't give

Miranda warnings, if they search places without cause or warrant, if they hold people without charges, if they bully or torture people into confessions, then you have to believe that the principle is more important, and the possible criminal has to go free. Being a liberal is damned hard. It requires you to not do what's expedient in the moment. It requires you to think long-term, to think ramifications, and to believe that ultimately good can come of it. But in the meantime, the comfort of black and white dims and the world can become awfully gray. Goddammit. Goddammit.

I knocked on Rhonda's door. She answered and invited me in. She was working on a paper, too, for her lit class. Mine was on Jonathan Swift and Rousseau. Hers was about John Milton and sin. I told her about my conversation with President Kelly. She started to yell at me, no quiet, wistful victim she. "So that motherfucker's getting away with it. That motherfucker," she shouted, and my chest felt tight and I could feel a brick swelling in my throat.

"I'm sorry. I'm sorry," I said, swallowing a sob.

She told me to leave, exclaiming that she'd sue, she'd get her parents to sue. She'd sue me. She'd sue the paper, the school, everyone. I don't know if she or her parents ever did. I was never contacted. I never spoke to Rhonda again.

Over the next few weeks, the bursar's office would be robbed at gunpoint in broad daylight and I would have to dive behind a trash can to avoid the shootout between the robber and cops before the masked guy carjacked a woman and drove off. That was my next scoop. Off-campus, a female student would be raped and murdered in her apartment. On campus, a male student in my dorm would drop bad acid and, in the kind of thing you only see in the movies, he would walk naked out onto the ledge of his seventh floor room, insisting he could fly before he leaped off. He didn't fly. He landed on the bike rack. He died on the way to the hospital.

His roommate was given straight A's and sent home for the remainder of the waning semester. It became a joke in our dorm that, if, say, one was studying for an exam and it was just too hard, one would say to one's roommate, "That's it. I'm throwing you out the window." I said it repeatedly to mine. 🅿

SIX CONSERVATIVE TALK RADIO HOSTS YOU MIGHT NOT KNOW

WE'RE GOIN' COAST-TO-COAST, live, all across the U.S. of A. in search of loathsome Limbaugh wannabes and Beck butt buddies. Like everyone else, each of these mike-suckin' buckets of hair is available for listening on your >

internets of insanity. They're big-time motivated by fears of other races and gay people and their "agendas." Now, you might think that the agenda of any group is just to be treated fairly, but, oh, no. Remember: If gay people adopt, Jesus will cry tears of blood. Or something like that. Who knows? I'm just making shit up. Like they are.

Remember: Every day, millions of Americans are listening to these liars and manipulators, believing that they are getting unvarnished reality. They don't get the attention of Laura Ingraham or Sean Hannity, and therefore mostly get to spout unchallenged, except in the most extreme of cases. If that doesn't scare you in the abstract, then enjoy the specifics:

MICHAEL BERRY

The top-rated local talker in Houston, Michael Berry has a JD from the University of Texas, a master's in law from the University of Nottingham—yes, that Nottingham, where sheriffs capture men in tights. This is not a stupid man, except that he is. For instance, regarding the possibility of a mosque—actually, a Muslim community center— being built near the site of the former World Trade Center in New York City, he opined, "I'll tell you this—if you do build a mosque, I hope somebody blows it up.... I hope the mosque isn't built, and if it is, I hope it's blown up, and I mean that." He later apologized for desiring an explosion in downtown Manhattan.

Berry has adopted a child from Ethiopia, which means he's an expert on black stuff. So he said of the Obama administration: "The only old white guy in Obama's circle is Joe Biden, and he's the butt of even Obama's jokes. He's the token old white guy." And he wrote, "'Nigga' isn't universal, but it also isn't relegated to Klan rallies" in an extended essay defending a black teaching assistant who was fired for saying "Nigga, please" to a black student in a high school classroom. They're both black, see? So, obviously, in this matter, a white guy is best qualified to judge the situation and say that it doesn't matter.

MIKE DELGIORNO

There's one distinction Michael DelGiorno has over most of his conservative gabbers: This asshole was sued for defamation and lost. When he was a simple man spewing a heady mixture of nutzoid acid and Jesus jizz all over the airwaves in Tulsa, Oklahoma, DelGiorno repeatedly accused City Councilor Bill Christiansen of committing felonies in his business dealings. According to Christiansen, Del-Giorno "looked forward to the day he ruined me, and it was his job to say it over and over again until people believed it." DelGiorno and radio station KFAZ tried to hide behind the First Amendment, which was intended to allow people to freely speak the truth, not spout lies. The case was settled for an undisclosed sum of money plus (and this is kind of awesome) publicly aired retractions on KFAZ for ten business days. This is not to mention his being banned from Indian-run casinos and his home foreclosure. DelGiorno "left" the station before his contract was up.

But never fear: Like a pernicious malignancy, the removal of the tumor from one place on the airwaves didn't get rid of the cancer. DelGiorno is now on an even bigger station, Supertalk 99.7 FM in Nashville, Tennessee. There, he freely (and seriously) calls Barack Obama the "antichrist," says that people with Obama bumper stickers might face violence against them because "things could escalate from town hall meetings right to the streets," and believes that the federal government is going to "come to arrest you or kill you."

Not that it's particularly relevant, but DelGiorno, who places "follower of Christ" above being a husband and father, has a club foot. That doesn't make him evil in and of itself, but it makes him seem far more troll-like, or like mad Rumpelstiltskin, tearing himself in two when his true name was spoken.

ROGER HEDGECOCK

Despite the handicap of having a penis at the end of his name, Roger Hedgecock was once the mayor of San Diego, a place that really loves its Cock. They love their Cock so much that, after being mayor, they gave it a special place in front of microphone, where it could ejaculate conservatively (which means on your face, but not in your hair) for over twenty years.[1]

A despicable drop of hog drool, Hedgecock said on Twitter, "Democrats crave dead miners" in the wake of the 2010 West Virginia

---

1 In reality, San Diego really intensely disliked its Cock. He was elected mayor in 1983. In 1985, he resigned after being convicted on one count of conspiracy and a dozen counts of perjury in a case involving the financing of his campaign.

mine disaster that killed twenty-seven men. He used to be Rush Limbaugh's main guest host, like Joan Rivers to Johnny Carson, whenever Limbaugh had tickets to Viagra-sponsored Dominican boy-whore tours. Called to the big leagues to pinch hit, Hedgecock said things like, in 2006, "The murder rate in Baghdad, the people being killed in Baghdad, is lower than the murder rate of Washington, DC." That would be true if the murder rate in Baghdad weren't nearly ten times the murder rate in DC. And, because no asshole tastes as sweet as Limbaugh's asshole, Hedgecock also said he agreed with the man in 2004 that the depraved torture at Abu Ghraib was "a prank; this is like college; this is like fraternities; this is—this is just these people. This is how they were raised." Which, if you think about it, is actually probably true.

BOB LONSBERRY

A serial-divorcing (three times) and overbreeding (seven kids) Mormon who was a missionary, bringing the hope of Joseph Smith's hat and Brigham Young's hatred and violence to Navajo and Hopi reservations, Lonsberry is on the radio in two places: Rochester, NY, where he lives, and, surprise, surprise, Utah on Family Values Radio. And how does he get people to understand that Mormons are open-hearted and caring? By calling welfare a "cancer" and "rewarded sloth." By calling the black mayor of Rochester a "monkey" and an "orangutan." By unashamedly stating that his great-grandfather was a member of the KKK. Essentially, he is a racist dogfucker. Is there evidence he has fucked dogs? Not to my knowledge. But there is no evidence he hasn't fucked dogs.[2]

Oh, and he also hates women: "There is a story about, um, girls who got pregnant in high school, and they stay in high school and let's give them a special award and tell them how proud we are of 'em. Or we could tell them they should have left their frickin' pants on, right. Keep your legs together, uh, Sweet Cheeks and everything will be OK. See here is the deal: We will have a school where there will be fifty girls who graduate with honors, and there will be five girls who get pregnant. Who do we have the special program for? Who do we give

---

2 I am using conservative standards for undemonstrable allegations that are patently false but sound mega-evil.

the certificate to? Who do we put stories about in the paper and tell them how proud we are? Little-sister-take-your-pants-off-and-spread-your legs, that's who gets the certificate." Remember: three divorces.

JANET PARSHALL

Broadcasting for Moody Radio,[3] Parshall, a woman who is fond of pantsuits and little or no make-up, is really, really worried about the homosexuals. Everywhere she looks, she sees lesbians and gay men. She can't help herself. On CNN's *Larry King Live*, in 2006, talking about *Brokeback Mountain* and blaming Matthew Shepard for his murder, she said, "I think what we're witnessing, Larry, is the homo-sexualizing of America." Which probably means better drapes.

"Wait," you may be thinking, "rewind that for a second: She blamed who for what, now?" Just so you know that this isn't hyperbo-le, here's what Parshall said about the gay twenty-one-year-old who was beaten to death in Laramie, Wyoming:

"Well, there's a lot of questions about [Shepard's] background. Was he, in fact, coming—and this is no way, shape, or form, a justi-fication of what happened because it was wrong, wrong, and wrong. Let there be no ambiguity there. But, in reality, I understand that Matthew was somewhat of a person who hung around some of the gay bars and was coming on to some people. So, was he looking for trouble in all the wrong places? If I were his mom, I would have given him some counsel, 'Stay away from that kind of a lifestyle,' because there's a way that seems right on demand and the end therein is death, and, unfortunately, it cost Matthew his life."

Other than getting the facts of the case completely wrong and Parshall's use of biblical-sounding language ("the end therein is death"), well, it's just par for the course for Parshall, whose recent ra-dio shows have featured such topics as "how to extend Christ's love to those living the homosexual lifestyle" and "the federal lawsuit seeking to overturn California's ban of same-sex marriage" and a discussion with the head of the National Director of Parents and Friends of Ex-Gays. Spreading Christ's love apparently is intimately bound up in keeping the legs of gays and lesbians closed.

3 You know those Moody ministries and Bible colleges you see everywhere that kind of give you the creeps, even if you don't know why, but maybe it's because it just seems vaguely cultish? Yeah, they have a radio network.

Sussman loves caves. He crawls around in bat shit, rubbing it all over his body as he seeks crevices and caverns in darkness, the only light his own. The SussMan, the asshole Twitter moniker he condemned himself with, is on the air in San Francisco, so you can imagine he sees himself as some kind of Charlton Heston among the damned, dirty apes. Although, as poor, abused researcher Kristina said, "His physical appearance is an alarming blend of both the Professor and Gilligan." And he acts as if he's a little bit of each. For instance, he wants to debate Al Gore on climate change, saying he will demonstrate "how science has been willingly corrupted by activists with Ph.D.'s" and show "who stands to make billions of dollars off the global warming scam." Where these billionaire scientists have been hiding is one of the earth's great mysteries.

And he loves hisself a heapin' helpin' o' Uhmerka: "Yer dang tootin' I'm angry. It's called righteous indignation, deal with it. 'Cause I'm convinced of something, ladies and gentlemen, the more facts you know, the more conservative you will become. The more you travel around this world, the more patriotic you will become. This is God's greatest gift to planet Earth: THE UNITED STATES OF AMERICA, the beacon of freedom!"

God, of course, was frantically pointing at things all around, like doves and daffodils and the Himalayas, yelling, "Hello?" But then he stopped, realizing that anyone who uses *dang tootin'* without irony is a lost cause. ℞P

FORMER SPEAKER OF THE HOUSE

Newt Gingrich

Total fuckbag

Complete cunt

1980 > 1990 1991 1992 1993 1994 1995 1996 1997 1998 1999 2000 2001 2002 2003 2004 2005 2006 2007 2008 2009 2010

1980: His cancer-ridden first ex-wife, Jackie, on Gingrich visiting her in the hospital: "When he got there, he wanted to discuss the terms of the divorce while I was recovering from my surgery." Still got reelected that year.

1994: Proposed ending welfare to teenage mothers and using the money to build orphanages. Still criticized Democrats for "social engineering."

1994: Contract With America condemned the nation to years of bullshit conservative rhetoric masked as populism. That shift in how conservatives presented their polarizing, anti–working class beliefs is Gingrich's greatest "accomplishment."

1995: Shut down the federal government by not holding a budget vote, an act of hubris that ended up leading to Bill Clinton's reelection, Republican losses in Congress, and Gingrich's eventual ouster.

1997: Reprimanded by the entire House of Representatives for, among other things, lying to the Ethics Committee.

1998: Resigned from the House amid further ethics probes, Republican overreach on the Clinton impeachment, and general douchebaggery. His hubristic insanity reached a wretched peak when he said that, if Clinton was impeached and removed from office and then a President Al Gore pardoned Clinton, he'd make sure that Gore was impeached, too. Thus, because of the distraction of impeachment, Gingrich helped cause 9/11.

Post-1998: A bloated, egotistical reminder of everything depraved and awful in the GOP, writing worthless books, starting various PACs in order to line his pockets, appearing on television to offer dubious opinions, and threatening to run for president.

☞ **PREDICTION**

Like Palin, Newt Gingrich has to run for president. And, until everyone remembers, "Oh, wait, isn't that the bastard who condemned Bill Clinton for a blow job at the same time that he was banging a chick who wasn't his wife?" he has an honest shot at the nomination. Redemption is only for those who are worth redeeming.

**A SERIES OF PORTRAITS
FEATURING RIGHT-WING PUNDITS
DOING DISGUSTING THINGS**

ARI FLEISCHER AT SUNRISE (March 12, 2009):

Ari Fleischer awakens in the morning sucking down air like a drowning man surfacing in the middle of the ocean, like he's only got a couple of seconds to breathe until >

the next wave washes over him, until he's dragged down by the undertow. And then he remembers who he is and what his role is in this world. "Goddamn you, soul," he says to himself, for, whatever you want to call it—soul, conscience, Jiminy Motherfuckin' Cricket—these split seconds when it escapes are always the most ledge-gripping terrors. He shoves it back down, forgets about the ocean, and rises.

After a piss, he showers and shaves, quickly, so that he doesn't have to stare at his face in the mirror for too long. It's those times that he wishes he still wore glasses because then there was some buffer between himself and his reflection, which always talks back to him, forcing him to remember all the lies he was given to tell with a straight face, lies that he was told to speak as forcefully as gospel, and that he ran away from because he couldn't stand seeing himself on television every night, demanding that no one question the lies he himself refused to question. When one lives under the threat of Dick Cheney breaking into your house and cutting your kids' jugulars in front of you, one tends to do what one is told.

Clean and dressed, he grabs a cup of coffee and pads into his office to check his e-mail, get his talking points, read Drudge. He watches a clip of himself looking smilingly impatient on *Hardball* last night, when he told Chris Matthews, "But after September 11, having been hit once, how could we take a chance that Saddam might not strike again? And that's the threat that has been removed, and I think we're all safer with that threat being removed." He watches the entire segment. Goddamn, he thinks, that was kick-ass.

And then Skype pops up. It's Rove. Goddammit. He just got dressed. "Ari, put on the fuckin' cam," Rove barks. Fleischer pauses, which just makes Rove angrier. "C'mon, you doe-eyed dick, I know you're there." Fleischer puts the cam on and asks Rove what he wants, as if he doesn't already know since Rove is sitting there without pants on. "You know what I want, Ari. Do it. Do the Oval Office trick." Shit, Fleischer thinks. How many times is he gonna have to go through this? Ever since he first did it on command for George W. Bush's amusement, Rove has come at him again and again.

Offering no resistance, Fleischer carefully removes his slacks and folds them over the chair. He turns the computer around so that the cam can get him in the middle of the floor. He drops his underwear and sits bare-ass on the rug. In the corner of his eye, he catches the screen and sees Rove starting to fondle his AAA battery of a penis. With the dexterity of a circus performer, Ari Fleischer pulls his legs behind his head and starts to suck his own cock. Rove moans as the former press secretary deep throats his own joint, jerkily bobbing his head up and down. A few moments of this, accompanied by a bit of anxious anus fingering, and both men groan as they cum together, Rove onto his lap, Fleischer into his mouth. It would surprise almost no one to hear that he's a swallower. The low rumble of Rove's voice comes from the computer's speakers: "That was good, Ari, really good. Talk to you soon." And the video window is gone.

Fleischer gets up, sighs, and wipes himself off with a Kleenex. He debates brushing his teeth as he puts his underwear and pants back on, but instead he swirls his cold coffee around his mouth. He sits back down at his computer, a little proud that he can still get the old legs back there. He uses some Purell on his asshole-fingering hand. And just as he sits back down and gets ready to do some more research, another window pops up. It's Bush. Fleischer rolls his eyes. He wonders why he even bothers putting pants on some mornings.

Glenn Beck in Teabag Heaven (April 13, 2009):

Glenn Beck settles down to finally sleep. It has been a long day, an exhausting one, promoting his 9/12 Project, imploring people to protest the modest tax increase on the wealthy by joining in the April 15 tea parties all around the nation, calling for active but polite revolution, walking that high wire that he knows he's on as the leader of a burgeoning faux movement, balancing precariously between being a demagogic violent cult leader and a blustering buffoon, with people around him willing his fall to one side or the other or some merger of the two. Yes, after a day of that, Glenn Beck returned home for his night time routine: He smoked a little crystal meth, beat his kids for telling him not to beat them again, tied up his wife on the bed, shoved an enema up his ass and took a shit on her before jacking off in her hair, weepingly apologized while he untied her, downed a few Ambien, and headed to his office to watch burn-victim porn until he could stagger over to the couch and collapse at last. It's the little things that get him through the days.

His dream is so very joyous. It is already the 15th, and Beck senses that he's in Boston, surrounded by his followers, some merrily dressed in eighteenth-century costumes, big-titted women in bustiers and giant skirts, men with little pony tails or in white powder wigs and long coats, some imitating the founders—dressed as Samuel Adams or Ben Franklin—and others, an entire crowd, old and young, fat and skinny, holding signs praising Beck, demanding more teabags for justice, and there's Bill O'Reilly and Bill Hemmer and Sean Hannity, winking at him, telling him that it's okay that he's the Fox "news" star now. There's a giant banner that reads: "Teabagging for America." It had to be teabags. They're easier to carry than loose tea.

Humbled, a few tears coming down his face, he hoists a teabag into the air. It's Celestial Seasonings chamomile because, to Beck, in his dream there's something almost intolerably effete, no, faggy about it. Everyone, even the Fox people, raise their teabags. At the end of the wharf, where the original Boston Tea Party site is still being refurbished, Beck faces the water and says, "This is for you, Mister President. We teabag you in the name of the citizens of the United States," and he casts his teabag into the harbor. He turns back, ready to watch the others do the same, but when he sees the crowd again, a very, very different scene is laid out before him.

Instead of the proud 9/12ers, Glenn Beck sees dozens and dozens of people on their knees. Standing over them are ludicrously dressed men, in leather bondage gear, in perverse variations of button-down coats and breeches. There are obvious cross-dressers standing there. And all of them, every man standing, has his balls out. Not just out, but in the slurping mouths of the men and women on their knees in front of them. There's Neil Cavuto, with John Hancock's nuts bobbing in and out of his agape, lapping facehole, jacking himself off. O'Reilly's trying to tell Paul Revere how to put his balls in, but the old silversmith keeps shoving them in to shut O'Reilly up. There's Greta Van Susteren, bouncing up and down on a propped up dildo, sucking the twin orbs of a man in Betsy Ross drag. "Oh, God," Beck thinks, "oh, dear God, this is not what I meant at all." Crying now, he falls to his knees, yelling, "Please, stop the teabagging."

The sobbing Beck feels something rubbing on the top of his head and hears a voice saying, *"Yeſ, yeſ, yeſ."* Beck turns around, leans back, and sees a man in Revolutionary War-era garb with a large nose and short wig with his ballsack in his hand. He says, *"Aye, Beck, your pointy hair feelſ wonderful on my teſticleſ. Theſe are the timeſ that try men'ſ foulſ, you know."*

It dawns on Beck. "Thomas Paine?" The man bows, his nutsack swinging in front of Beck's face.

Paine gestures to his cold balls. *"Fir, thiſ iſ a teabag party, iſ it not? Then theſe bagſ are for you, ſir."*

"But, no, I can't..." Beck looks over and sees Sean Hannity fairly gobbling the balls of Benjamin Franklin. Catching him staring, Hannity gives Beck a thumbs up and goes back to work tongue-bathing Franklin's balls. Beck understands: This is what he has to do to make America safe.

So he gets his knees in a comfortable position and grimly, slowly, begins to lick Thomas Paine's balls. And, strangely, Beck discovers it's kind of fun, with Paine's hard cock rubbing the side of his face. Yes, yes, Glenn Beck decides that he likes teabagging. He likes the feel of patriot balls in his mouth. By God, he really loves balls. And he can feel himself getting an erection. This is great. A totally new sensation. And when Paine grabs him by his hair to make him slow his slobbering down a bit, Beck almost comes without touching himself. Indeed, this is a party now. A real teabag party. When one is concentrating on pleasuring a man's nuts, one forgets all about taxes and socialism and even God. The only cause is seeing how hot you can get those boys.

Beck's alarm goes off. He thinks for a moment about the comfort of having a mouthful of balls. He twitches a little, having to keep the meth desire in check for the day, and decides to get moving. Reality is reality, after all, and he's got a whole nation waiting for his orders.

Limbaugh in Afghanistan (A Fantasia with Apologies to Paul Bowles[1]):
Rush Limbaugh knew he shouldn't have trusted Ahmed, the local jirga member who told him to follow him outside the compound in Kandahar to see the endless poppy fields. Limbaugh wanted to confront his temptations, demonstrate he was a stronger man. Now he's lost in the ruins of an ancient mosque, alone, hungry, pissed off because he's due to be live on the radio in a couple of hours, bringing his faithful listeners tales of American triumphalism. How they admired him, how the soldiers even asked him if he was going to run for office. God, he felt somehow right and at home here, praising the good works of real Americans, deriding the milquetoast president who would even think about abandoning the noble mission to rid the country of the Taliban. Or something along those lines.

He hears the clatter of distant hoofsteps, across the rocky terrain. Finally, he thinks, some local to help him. They ride up to him, three men with scraggly beards and Chitrali hats. "Can you help me? I'm an American. American. I need to get back to Kandahar Air Base," he declares as the men on horses circle him slowly, speaking in a dialect that Limbaugh not only can't understand, but hasn't heard yet. They are surveying him. "I'm on the radio. You know the radio?" He makes some futile hand gesture of a microphone in front of his mouth, of holding a mike with his mouth open, pointing at it with his other hand, nodding and winking.

The horse-borne men look at each other and nod. Limbaugh smiles. The power of Excellence in Broadcasting, no doubt. Americans are saving them from the Taliban and now he will receive their thanks. One of them says something to Limbaugh, and as the radio host turns towards that horse, another man clubs Limbaugh in the back of his head. Limbaugh hits the ground with all the grace of an oversized turd being shat out of a constipated elephant.

The Pashtun men pick up the porcine pundit and stuff him into a large bag, carrying him between two horses back into the mountains. When they get back to their village, a small compound really, of men only and a few younger boys, they spill Limbaugh out and leave him to regain consciousness, one of the boys watching over him.

Limbaugh comes out of his haze and bellows, "I'll call the fuckin' embassy." The boys run off as Limbaugh continues to yell, "There's gonna be hell to pay when the Americans hear of this. We'll fuckin' eat your hearts and minds." A couple of the men enter the shack and walk over to him. He thrashes and screams, "We're gonna bomb you back beyond the stone age, you raghead—"

[1] Yeah, yeah, I know that Paul Bowles wrote about North Africa, not Afghanistan. But go with it.

But one of the men has grabbed Limbaugh's tongue and, with one swift slice of a dagger, cuts it off. Stunned and tasting his own metallic blood, Limbaugh falls back on his thin mattress of rugs and another man tears his sleeve and shoots him up with the purest heroin anyone can get. Limbaugh fades to black.

He comes in and out, occasionally gargling a word or two, occasionally feeling the fever of infection that's come over him, occasionally feeling the warm sting of the needle. Once he feels an incredible pain between his legs, seeing men above him, but he passes out again. Finally, a ragged, shit-stained Limbaugh staggers out of the shack one day as the sun shines around him. He unzips his pants to take a piss. He reaches in and notices an absence below his tiny penis. He's been castrated. He screams in outrage.

Quickly, several men rush up to him and wrap tin bands around his arms, his legs, his waist. Limbaugh is confused until he realizes that each band contains several bells and as he moves around he makes a clattering, ringing sound that seems to please the Pashtun men watching him. He forgets about his lost balls for a second and finds this curious. He takes a couple of steps, ringing the bells as he moves, and the men clap and ululate in approval. Limbaugh smiles and nods. Even Pashtun nutcutters recognize talent when they see it.

Limbaugh becomes popular in the villages around Zaranj, a favorite of the women and children, who watch in separate audience, as Limbaugh dances, horribly, for them, ringing his bells. He learns to do handstands and high kicks and twirls. Oh, what a happy clown, the children think. Limbaugh learns how to scare the women by growling and barking. And then, when he performs for the men, they drum and play instruments, and he becomes just another member of the band. If you're going to be the plaything of the tribe of some warlord, at least the food's regular (if tasteless) and the audiences are appreciative.

Limbaugh doesn't even mind the fact that every night he's locked up in a room with no window. He doesn't even mind the regular sodomizings by the Pashtun men, the ones who hadn't earned a boy yet. Limbaugh misses his voice, though, and some nights he cries in remembrance of his silver-tipped tongue, his quick wit now inward only. He thinks he's even forgotten how to write. But then he gets his nightly dose of smack and he's in bliss until the sun rises again.

One day his keepers bring him to a village on the edge of a poppy field, and there it is: that sea of red flowers, the pinprick bloodlets growing from the earth. Against the setting sun, it looks like a fire that would finally consume him. The last anyone sees of Rush Limbaugh is a silhouetted figure, bells ringing, running into the field of flames, grunting happily, leaping madly. **RP**

"I" PROPOSAL FOR A BOOK ON
ANN COULTER THAT I BAILED ON

BACK IN 2006, I was approached by a publisher to write a book about Ann Coulter with the help of a Well-Known Journalist Whom I Admire. For a few days, I contemplated the possibilities and came up with the following proposal:

"One cannot write about Ann Coulter without >

writing about the phenomenon that has been manufactured around her. In my blog, the Rude Pundit, I have written many times, in quite vicious terms, about Coulter's ability to incite anger with statements that are lies, insults, or just outright bigotry. Yet, no matter how much of that is pointed out, her fans (and the people who make money off her) unquestioningly support her, living up to

the larger version of the word *fanatics*. And her bomb-throwing gets her constantly invited on just about every talk show out there, from the expected Fox "news" programs to CNBC economic chat shows to the *Tonight Show*. Perhaps she'll show up on *Sesame Street* to mock Bert and Ernie for living together.

"The book, then, would be both an investigative biography and a first-person journey into the cult of Coulter. In alternating chapters, I would lay out her life story and then use her as a way of exploring the culture of rabidly right-wing America. For example, one chapter would examine her rise from attorney to media star in the wake of the Paula Jones case and Bill Clinton's impeachment. And in the next chapter, I would have a running commentary on watching hours of Coulter appearances on television (yes, I am willing to do this for the public good).

"A chapter on her early life and her writings while at Cornell would be followed by a trip through the world of her fans, including interviews with people where she is speaking, as well as Internet sites and chat rooms devoted to her. Of course, that would be contrasted with a look at those who hate Coulter, too, in order to be fair and balanced. Another chapter would be something like 'Walking a Mile in Ann's Ferragamos,' where I visit the Manhattan church she claims to attend, the town in Florida where she is registered to vote (and the town where she actually has a house), and more places indicated by her writings and interviews.

"From the marketing of Coulter to her approach to research in her writing to critiques of her views to her hair, legs, and alleged Adam's apple, the book will be a humorous, biting, well-researched, and serious look at someone whose very mention causes polarizing reactions in people. The book will place Coulter in her times, as both a cause and effect of the divisiveness wrought by the conservative movement. The book will be devoted to answering a few questions: 1) Does she really believe what she says? 2) How many people take her seriously? and 3) What does the attention accorded Ann Coulter say about the larger American political landscape?

"Ann Coulter is a symptom and a disease. I hope to write a book that treats both."

I was getting ready to start writing when I realized, "I would rather be raped by a tiger than give up a year of my life for the sake of that kooz." And, short story short, I didn't write the book. The lesson? Fuck her. RP

**TEN REALLY AWFUL
AND MOSTLY SEXIST THINGS
I DON'T REGRET WRITING
ABOUT ANN COULTER**

I've been truly, terribly mean to Ann Coulter, and I'd feel bad, if she wasn't such a cunt.[1] >

---

1 I understand this push-button word. However, if brevity is the soul of wit, then "cunt" is the wittiest and most apt word available in the English language to describe Coulter.

1. You could be standing neck deep in a shit-filled sewer, covered with syphilis sores and shoving a crucifix up your ass, and you'd still have the moral high ground over Ann Coulter.

2. Facts are to Ann Coulter as coyote piss is to deer.

3. If she was some fat, bald guy with no fellatio abilities living in a tiny apartment in Idaho and writing these things, she'd've been arrested a long time ago.

4. Chances are Ann Coulter's anorexic or, at the very least, bulimic, considering the number of times she's referred to Monica Lewinsky and Hillary Clinton as "chubby." And in that case, we can expect a peaking of madness as her weight drops, followed, perhaps, by a brain hemorrhage that keeps her in a coma until she finally dies under the burden of her own rot.

5. When is she going to end up coked out of her mind, swinging on a pole in a strip club in, say, Elizabeth, New Jersey, shovin' her little titties in men's faces for a buck, and when she offers her opinion on, say, the war, the good truck-drivin' vets'll say, "You know, you'd be a lot prettier with my cock in your mouth"?

6. Coulter likes to use ribbed dildos made of puppy spines in a vain attempt to get some feeling in her calloused clit.

7. I wouldn't fuck her if I was given Rush Limbaugh's tiny, diseased prick to fuck her with.

8. Bitch has been ridden hard and put away spooge-covered, taken out the next day, stiff and sticky, and spit on to be cleaned up for her interviews before using her to wipe Republican asses.

9. Fuck her and her brute of a father. He's in hell now, alongside Reagan and McCarthy, getting raped by barbed-dick demons with his daughter's face.

10. Attempting to find logic in Ann Coulter's writing is not un-akin to trying to finger-fuck a porcupine's asshole. :P

FIVE TIMES ANN COULTER CALLED FOR PEOPLE TO DIE OR MOCKED THE DEAD[1]

1. In reference to Dr. George Tiller, who was murdered by anti-abortion activist Scott Roeder: "I am personally opposed to shooting abortionists, but I don't want to impose my moral values on others."

2. In reference to the white nationalist who bombed the Murrah Federal Building in Oklahoma City: "My only regret with Timothy McVeigh is he did not go to the *New York Times* Building."

3. In reference to Democrat John Edwards's mention of his son's automobile accident: "If you want points for not using your son's death politically, don't you have to take down all those 'Ask me about my son's death in a horrific car accident' bumper stickers?"

3a. In reference to her implication that Edwards is a "faggot": "If I'm gonna say anything about John Edwards in the future, I'll just wish he had been killed in a terrorist assassination plot."

4. In reference to the death of Howard Dean's brother: "Bizarrely, after working on the failed George McGovern campaign, Charlie Dean went to Indochina in 1974 to witness the ravages of the war he had opposed. Not long after he arrived, the apparently ungrateful communists captured and killed him. *Hey fellas! I'm on your s— CLUNK!*"

5. In reference to President Bill Clinton: "In this recurring nightmare of a presidency, we have a national debate about whether he 'did it,' even though all sentient people know he did. Otherwise there would be debates only about whether to impeach or assassinate."

---

1 She'd probably say it's all just jokes, ha-ha, and that we can't take it. No, we can take the jokes. They're just not funny.

NAKED RIGHT-WINGER HOUSE

M E M O
to HBO or Showtime

Re:
New Television Series

Dear Big TV Executives,

I'd like to come to
your offices in either
Hollywood or New York,
whichever is more
convenient for you. >

I wanna pitch some producer a show, a reality series, you know, like *So You Think You Can Dance?* or *Check Out These Whores.* I'm gonna call the show *Naked Right-Wing Media House,* and it'll be a bit more esoteric than, say, your run of the mill *Amazing Race* or *Let's All Get Herpes* kinds of shows. See, what I wanna do is gather a whole bunch of conservative media people, commentators, writers, just a mess of 'em, like Rush Limbaugh and Bill O'Reilly and Glenn Beck and Sean Hannity and William Kristol and Michael Savage and Joe Scarborough, and we'll put 'em all in a house, a big motherfucker of a house, with a kitchen and lots of bathrooms and a bunch of flat-screen TVs, real nice-like, 'cause that's what our man-o'-the-people right-wing pundits expect. The twist is this: They can't wear clothes. Not a stitch. Bare-ass, ball-dangling, hard-nipple naked.

So—go with me on this—we'll fill the place, making nude roomies of Steve Doocy and George Will. And for the first week, we'll just check 'em out, watching how they deal with each other, with some of the guys openly checkin' out the dicks of the other right-wingers, maybe with them forming cock-size cliques, with Glenn Beck by himself because he thinks he has a big dick, but it's really just plain and average and stupid, and no one wants him as part of their group, except O'Reilly keeps asking Beck to let him stand close so his own prick doesn't look as tiny. We'll see how naked columnists act, if Matt Drudge spends his time grooming himself, plucking hairs off his ass, if Charles Krauthammer tries to show Kristol how to make his balls look bigger by squeezing them.

Yes, yes, what fun. Lots of it, with all kinds of moments where we see Andrew Breitbart taking a gigantic, moaning shit, where we smile when Brit Hume and Neil Cavuto accidentally touch cocks while passing each other in the hallway. Jesus, the ratings'll go through the fucking roof. Are you listening, HBO?

Now, here's the twist. We're not gonna vote anyone off. Oh, no. What we'll do is each week, just remove a room or two from the house. Just cut it off and wall it up. One day it's two to a bedroom, next day it's three. One day it's two to a bathroom, next day it's four. We'll be slow about it, building the inexorable, "holy fuck, they wouldn't do that, would they?" tension up. Sure, sure, at first, it'll just be all comical tension and mismatched roomies and little tensions and spats, with Limbaugh forcing Doocy and Tucker Carlson to put on bronze make-up and dance together with their cocks shoved between their legs so they look like a couple of Dominican teen hookers. Over in the corner will be Pat

Buchanan, weeping because he wants to jack off so badly, but he thinks it's a sin. The toilets'll overflow. They'll have to learn to work together or fall apart.

And that's fine and dandy for a couple of weeks. But then we'll get rid of more and more rooms, until there's only one bedroom, one bathroom, one kitchen, and one TV in the single living room. And then we'll throw the women in—Ann Coulter and Michelle Malkin and Peggy Noonan and S. E. Cupp and a random assortment of replaceable Fox "news" blondes. They'll be naked, too, of course. So that even if they've decided to be a team, the naked male right-wingers, the straight ones at least, will now have to deal with the sight of pussy staring them in the face, of tits laying next to them, and then all hell will break loose as the men try to claim their women, as the women try to maintain their independence.

And then we'll get rid of the bathroom.

That's right. All of a sudden, the naked right-wingers will have to shit and piss in front of each other, on the furniture, in the sink. Maybe they'd segment off the bedroom as the designated latrine, but then we'll get rid of that.

There the naked right-wingers will be, covered in each other's excrement and urine, unable to bathe, sticking together, sliding against each other. God, who could care at that point if Dennis Miller is buggering Laura Ingraham. If Frank Luntz is blowing Karl Rove. Who could tell?

And we'll get rid of the kitchen. And all the food will be gone. Vanished. Poof.

Who will eat whom first? 'Cause no one's leaving this damn house, right? No one's getting out. You gotta start with the fat ones, so Limbaugh, Buchanan, and Maggie Gallagher are ham, bacon, and roast beef. Then, on principle, Glenn Beck would be eviscerated and roasted on a spit in the middle of the living room. Yes, by the end, the right-wingers would be reduced to shit-covered primitive beasts slaughtering each other until the last ones die of disease or starvation. My money's on either Coulter or G. Gordon Liddy being the final right-winger to die.

But, you may ask, isn't this a game? Who wins?

Oh, c'mon. Who do you think?

So let's set up a meeting where we can begin to work out a contract and budget details. The sooner, the better.

Sincerely,

The Rude Pundit ℞

**WALTER CRONKITE IN PURGATORY
(A FANTASIA)**

IT'S NOT THAT WALTER CRONKITE NECESSARILY EXPECTED to go straight to Heaven after he died. No, he was used to being consigned to a vast, empty, middle space, having thought upon his retirement that, surely, CBS News would >

rely upon him as a kind of anchor emeritus. Instead, he was abandoned like an incontinent dog whose owners didn't have the time to care for it. Done in by the very bastards he had elevated, told he was a fossil against the evolved, snappy shallowness of the news on ABC, he could at least comfort himself that he outlasted David Brinkley. And then, because he still had some things he wanted to say, Walter Cronkite did hour-long documentaries for the wasteland of barely viewed cable stations, the kinds of things that the decimated network news bureaus used to do and that a public, who at least pretended to give a shit, watched.

So Cronkite was used to Purgatory. And when his soul stalled in an empty room, he knew he wasn't in Hell. But it wasn't Heaven. He figured he had a few sins to answer for. That time he broke Harry Reasoner's nose with a martini shaker when that son of a bitch stole an interview slot with Kissinger. That evening he spent masturbating in a corner while watching Ed Murrow madly ball Vivian Vance at the Plaza after a network banquet. That time he nude oil wrestled Chet Huntley for the deranged pleasures of Pat Weaver and William Paley. That weekend in Cape Cod with Barbara Walters where they never even saw the ocean. That tormenting thought that if he had opposed the Vietnam War even sooner, in 1967, in 1966, that it could have saved lives. Cronkite's conscience never let him rest while on Earth. Why would it in the afterlife?

The final straw for him was the coverage of the death of Michael Jackson. As he saw everyone who ever considered themselves a real journalist actually spend time, as if a president or civil rights leader had passed, delving into the death of another drug addict whose presence in the world had dwindled to a mere freak show burp in the wind was too much. There was no reason for him to be alive anymore. As he let himself die, he mourned not himself, but his profession. As degraded as it had become, one of the hopes after the September 11, 2001, attacks was that the news found its purpose again, that the brain-numbing concentration on gossip and bullshit like the Chandra Levy death was going to be consigned to the back pages, that the press was going to retake its place as an unacknowledged check and balance.

But between the corporatization and concentration of the media and the uncritical reporting of the march to the Iraq War, the hyping of American bloodlust, when he had said, so very clearly, that such things were futile, assured the death of his kind of journalism. It's not that glorification of crime, violence, and celebrity, and the luscious mixture of them, didn't exist during his time. But those were blips, not the *raison d'etre* of the news. They were occasional indulgences that lasted a day, not the bread and butter that fed the news cycle.

Still, though, Cronkite couldn't understand the purpose in the fact that his room in Purgatory was filled with televisions showing all the talking heads, all O'Reilly, Beck, Maddow, Olbermann, Hannity, Matthews, Grace, Sanchez, and more, every anchor on every twenty-four-hour news network, none of them offering anything without commentary, none of them simply giving us the news, all of them spinning and breaking facts to suit their ideas and agendas, whether alone or with guests. Cronkite wanted to know why he should be forced to see this, these pretenders who would never command the respect he had had, let alone the numbers.

Three years of this, of the undying thrum of editorial masked as news, and he finally got it. He had to admit it: His proudest moment was also the beginning of the death of news. It wasn't just the corporate culture and the merging of commercial and press concerns. He had to say that his declaration of the Vietnam War as "unwinnable" was also his greatest sin. His outrage mainstreamed subjectivity. He had to accept that in order to get out of Purgatory and finally see Betsy again.

But not just that. No, that would be too simple, and God is nothing if not a tricky motherfucker. What Cronkite realized was that to just accept that he is one of the reasons that all television news now wears its biases as badges of honor would be to give in to those who had attacked him for turning on the war. He also had to understand the sin and then say he would do the same thing all over again. That it was both a betrayal of the trust he had built up and his sacred duty because of that very trust. His job was to report the news, yes, but it wasn't to watch idly as the leaders of the nation sent kids to death. So take the good with the bad. If Bill O'Reilly was the result, so be it.

As the room around him began to disappear, as his ascension began, Cronkite was mournful, because he had opened the floodgates. But he didn't make the flood. Johnson did. Nixon did. He merely tried, as best he could, in the only way he knew, to alleviate the damage. **RP**

MISSISSIPPI GOVERNOR

Haley Barbour

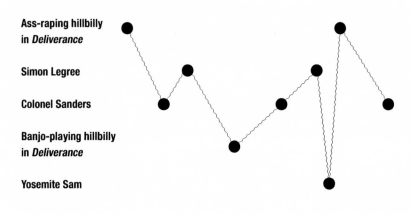

Ass-raping hillbilly in *Deliverance*

Simon Legree

Colonel Sanders

Banjo-playing hillbilly in *Deliverance*

Yosemite Sam

1982 > 1990 1991 1992 1993 1994 1995 1996 1997 1998 1999 2000 2001 2002 2003 2004 2005 2006 2007 2008 2009 2010

1982: When he ran for Senate, an aide told him that there would be "coons" at an event. According to the *New York Times*, Barbour said that "if the aide persisted in racist remarks, he would be reincarnated as a watermelon and placed at the mercy of blacks." One imagines that Barbour did not put it quite so tactfully.

1991: Founded powerful lobbying firm which got powerfuller and richer by lobbying for Big Tobacco (to the tune of $3.8 million from 1998 to 2002 alone).

1993: Became chair of the Republican National Committee. He did a great job in getting Republicans to control Congress, thus assuring us nonstop investigations of the Clinton administration and enough distractions to prevent the United States from killing or capturing Osama bin Laden. So, yes, Haley Barbour caused 9/11.

1997: Resigned as chair in order to make tobacco companies look good.

2001: Lobbying for utilities, he thought the Bush/Cheney administration was too strict on carbon emissions.

2004: Became Governor of Mississippi because no one expected a white man whose voice sounds like Foghorn Leghorn gargling balls would win.

2005: Behaved relatively honorably during the aftermath of Hurricane Katrina

2006: Won a court battle to defund a highly successful anti-smoking program targeted at kids.

2010: Kept telling people that the media and federal government were overreacting and to visit Mississippi's beaches until the day BP oil spill tar balls washed ashore. Then he demanded federal help.

☞ **PREDICTION**

Prediction: No one with this long a résumé is ever, ever going to be elected president, although enough people owe him that either they're gonna have to support his nomination or literally suck his cock. The best case scenario is that he dies of lung cancer.

MINNESOTA GOVERNOR

Tim Pawlenty

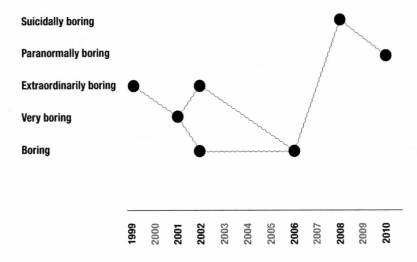

1999: As Minnesota House Majority Leader, said of Governor Jesse "The Body" Ventura's venture back into the wrestling ring, "I think there's room in politics for some good humor and fun, but I think this really crossed a line.... You had to watch it to understand just how low this thing has sunk...the degradation of women, the violence, the rituals, the swearing."

2001: Was about to announce a run for Senate when Karl Rove and Dick Cheney called him and, after Cheney threatened to forced-feed his testicles to his children if he ran, he stepped back and supported Norm Coleman.

2002: Elected governor in a four-way race with 44.4 percent of the vote.

2003: "Over a 14-month period, while Pawlenty was a sitting legislator and active candidate for governor, he was paid by a [telecom] company with significant interest in legislative and regulatory policies—and no one but his close political allies knew about it. And he can't say with any specificity what he did for his pay."

2006: Reelected governor in a three-way race with 46.7 percent of the vote. Despite never having cracked 50 percent in his state, he thinks he can run for president.

2008: Vetoed a 7.5-cent-a-gallon state gas tax to pay for bridge and highway repair, even after the I-35W Mississippi River Bridge collapsed, killing thirteen people. Bonus points: Pardoned a convicted child molester because he married his victim when she was old enough to consent.

2010: In a move that degraded women more than any wrestling match ever had, declared April "Abortion Recovery Month," where the governor insisted that women had to feel bad about getting still (for now) legal abortions.

☞ **PREDICTION**

Despite having a record of being occasionally reasonable on issues like children's health care (remember: it's the one progressive thing it's always okay to take care of), Pawlenty has veered so hard to the right that it's as if his left side has had a stroke. Crazy it up as he might, 2012 is gonna be like 2001, with his hand shaking every time the phone rings and his caller ID shows it's Rove's number. And did I mention how awfully boring he is?

★
★
★
★
★
★

Part 6:

THE SOLSTICE: BACK TO LOUISIANA, AGAIN, AGAIN & AGAIN

**FREE SPEECH
DOESN'T MEAN NICE SPEECH**

AT THE UNIVERSITY OF SOUTHWESTERN LOUISIANA IN THE 1980S,

the Bayou Bijou movie theater in the campus center was the only place in Lafayette where an art house film would play. If you wanted to see any foreign film at >

all, your Bergmans or your Kurosawas, you had to hope it got programmed into the smallish auditorium. Sometimes the film committee rose to the occasion and brought in a movie before it was on the fast track to VHS or late night on Showtime.

So it was that when the Bayou Bijou announced that it was going to show Jean-Luc Godard's film *Hail Mary*, we proud wannabe cinephiles were thrilled. Not only would we get a Godard film right when it came out, but this one was gonna fuck with people. *Hail Mary* reimagines the story of the Virgin Mary in contemporary France, featuring a constantly horny Joseph, a street thug angel Gabriel, and a basketball-playing Mary who masturbates while quoting Kierkegaard. The local churches were upset as hell, which was half the fun.

And then the university's administration pulled the plug and canceled the showing. It was one of those idiotic moves that people in power do in order to shut up the loudest asshole in the room. I imagine the meeting went like this:

Catholic high-muckety-muck with a big hat: "JESUS SAD! JESUS SMASH! JESUS NO ALLOW US TO GIVE MONEY TO CAPITAL CAMPAIGN!"

Eye-rolling administrator who just wants to be left the fuck alone: "Okay, shit, whatever, Your Highness, we'll stop the damn film."

Catholic muckety-muck (hat nodding): "Jesus happy. Now me go rape altar boy."

I should probably point out here that one of the first major Catholic Church scandals involving a molesting priest and a cover-up by a diocese was the Father Gilbert Gauthe case. In 1984, Gauthe was arrested for assaulting eleven boys and later admitted to molesting twenty-six more in churches all around Lafayette Parish.[1] The court case was just wrapping up in 1986 as the Godard film controversy took off the next year. So, in other words, right after the Catholic Church was ordered to pay sexual assault victims $22 million in compensation, it was worried that showing a movie with Mary's pubes on display would damage people's souls.

Needless to say, as a columnist and arts editor for the school paper, *The Vermilion*, I was outraged at the administration, most especially at the dean of students, Raymond Blanco, who was married (and still is) to future (now ex-) Louisiana Governor Kathleen Blanco. He was the designated fall guy to cast aside the concerns of liberal little students and faculty due to his ability to

---

1 It's estimated, though, that he had over a hundred victims.

remain unflappable and buoyant, no matter the criticism. I interviewed him for an article and his defense was, "You don't understand these things," a bald assertion of power. I was a graduating senior, so my attitude was "Fuck him," and I went on the attack, as did the entire paper.

We wrote columns. We got the faculty involved. Could there be a more clear infringement of First Amendment rights? You got speech squelched, you got religion established, you got assembly halted, all on property that received federal money. It was pretty goddamned obvious. Eventually, the faculty senate passed a unanimous condemnation of the act. The administration negotiated with the faculty and agreed that the film could play the next fall, but not in the movie theater. It had to be in a large auditorium classroom with a panel of professors speaking about religion, film, and the First Amendment afterward. In other words, it had to be an academic event, not a cinematic one.

I should probably point out here that, every year, the Bayou Bijou's biggest film event was the single porno it would show at the end of the spring semester. And it wasn't R-rated soft-core shit you see on Cinemax. Oh, no. This was cum shot and penetration porn, with cocks and cunts aplenty. I had a magical night watching the disturbingly hot and hotly disturbing *Café Flesh*. There was never a peep of protest.[2]

In the summer between that spring and the following fall, when I started grad school, *Hail Mary* came out on video. I gathered friends and we watched the transgressive act by a bold cinematic innovator. So, like, have you ever seen the movie? 'Cause it's fucking boring. And we weren't stoned or anything. It was an awful experience, a pretentious bunch of bullshit. We were pissed and more than a little bemused that we had spent a good chunk of time battling for a movie that maybe ten people would stay and watch.

This ain't a Godard film, so I won't pause here to touch myself and ruminate on the nature of fate and experience or anything. I'll jump cut, Michael Bay–style, motherfuckers, to the action.

Night of the showing. October 1988. It was in the English building at USL, where my office was. Everyone asked me during the day if I was going to it. "No," I answered, "because it fucking sucks. But I'll come to the forum after." As I drove up to the building, I saw a group of protesters chanting outside. It was mostly one church group, but they were an enthusiastic bunch, with posters about offending God and going to hell. The usual m.o. I walked past them, through the doors, noticed that the auditorium classroom was getting filled, and headed around the corner to my office.

2 A couple of years after I graduated, the porn film tradition ended. It was a sad day, filled with much flaccidity all over campus. A lonely blow-up doll, eyes wide like saucers, was tossed into the campus swamp (note: there's a swamp on campus), floating in protest until a squirrel jumped on it and stored an acorn in its mouth.

Grading papers or writing a paper, I don't remember, I awaited the end of the flick. At some point, I heard singing. I walked over to the glass front doors and saw all of the protesters on their knees. I turned to the campus security guy, who was staring at them in the light leaking from the building. "That's really annoying," I said.

"They started when the movie started. They say they're gonna pray until it's over," he offered. I nodded and went back to my office.

When *Hail Mary* was done, I met my friend Toby and we headed into the auditorium, which was nearly full. A couple of hundred people. Had it just played at the Bayou Bijou without a peep, there might have been twenty-five audience members. We sat about halfway down; on stage, four or five professors, including several we had or were taking, arranged themselves along a table.

After a few minutes of talk about freedom of speech, about the administration's poor decisions, the floor was opened for questions. An old man carrying one of the protest signs stood up and started asking about how the campus could be allowed to show the movie. He began to get all Jesus-y for a moment, but not crazy Jesus-y. He was early in his comments when someone else in the room called out to him, "Did you watch the movie?"

This flustered the old guy, who barked back, "No, I don't have to see it to know—"

He was cut off by others there starting to yell things like, "Shut up." The old man started to get agitated as the crowd booed at him.

I turned to Toby. "Um, isn't this supposed to be about free speech?"

With the old man yelling in the background, trying to continue his point, Toby shrugged. "I guess only for some." I looked at the faculty on stage, who were not doing anything.

Finally, the campus cops came in and dragged the old man away to the cheers of the crowd. "That was... bullshit," I said to Toby, who agreed. For the rest of the Q&A, during this event that had happened, to some extent, because of my actions, I kept kicking myself for not standing up for that old man, for not standing there, amid the derision, and saying that what had happened was wrong and that we should be ashamed. But I hadn't. And so I was complicit in denying the man his right to speak.

At the end of the forum, Toby and I went up to Bob Gramling, a sociology prof who had led the evening. We said we wanted to talk to him about the old man, about how it had bothered us. "Yeah, that was pretty fucked up," Gramling said. "I thought about stopping the cops, but it was their call."

"It kind of made the night into a joke," I said. Gramling sadly nodded his head, but there was no answer to be had. And the whole thing ended with us silently walking away. ⬤P

FOUR MONTHS AFTER HURRICANE KATRINA, just before New Year's Eve 2005, I went to different areas of metro New Orleans. What I saw was a vibrant, alive, breathing city transformed into a necropolis. >

I took pictures and I took my brother, Gary, who supported George W. Bush in two elections.

Slidell, Louisiana, about twenty miles outside New Orleans, on the north shore of Lake Pontchartrain:

A couple of photos from the Lower Ninth Ward in New Orleans, where every-thing looked like the week after the water receded:

Slidell:

The old Check In/Check Out didn't make it. I had used the promise of a po'
boy from that gas station turned beacon of fried seafood sandwichdom as an
enticement to get my brother to go along on a trip to the New Orleans area.
Surely, I thought, having heard about how so much of Slidell was fine, the
Check In/Check Out would have made it. But, like so much else you heard
about recoveries then, it's all relative. It's like saying that if we discover mi-
crobes on Mars, we've discovered aliens. Well, yeah, technically, but, c'mon, we
were promised little green men.

Slidell was a divided city—an obvious line where the floods from Lake
Pontchartrain ended extended across a large swath of the town. On one side,
there was a kind of normalcy, as if no gigantic storms had passed right over the
North Shore. On the other, there was a continuing degradation of the buildings of the town as you rode from I-12 down to the boarded-up businesses of
Front Street and finally to the absolute destruction of the area approaching the
Highway 11 bridge across the lake. At the Starbucks on the corner of Pontchartrain and Front, people waited for FEMA officials to talk to them about flood
insurance, for insurance agents to talk to them about other kinds.

I headed into the neighborhoods where there were the now-former
homes of people I knew who no longer lived there. During the ride to Slidell,
I had passed at least a dozen trucks towing FEMA trailers, and in this
subdivision, many of them were parked on lawns outside of houses, some
with Christmas decorations on them. And when I say, "houses," I mean it in
the sense of structure, for every house—every house—was gutted to the studs
and foundation. The dirt in front of the homes, which used to be covered
by "lawns," held either the enormous piles of debris, the ruined furniture,
decorations, possessions, sheetrock, carpeting, that used to fill the houses;
or all the detritus of the carried-away debris, life reduced to bits of trash,
a broken CD, the pages of a book. My brother noticed a page in the dirt
outside of the house of some of my friends: It was titled "The Mystery of
Atlantis."

It was much the same in subdivision after subdivision, with shopping
centers and churches still merely wrecked shells with piles of garbage outside
them. Some churches held services in tents, some in smaller spaces. In the
wealthier area of Eden Isles, a similar destruction had occurred, although most
of the homes had second stories, which were able to be occupied. Outside of one
gutted home, a perfectly clean infinity pool was in working order, complete with

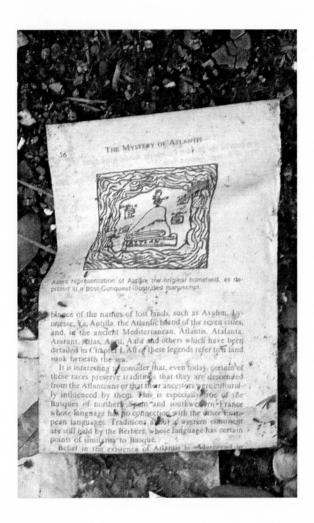

THE MYSTERY OF ATLANTIS

Aztec representation of Aztlan, the original homeland, as depicted in a post-Conquest illustrated manuscript.

...blance of the names of lost lands, such as Avalon, Lyonesse, Ys, Antilia, the Atlantic island of the seven cities, and, in the ancient Mediterranean, Atlantis, Atalanta, Atarant, Atlas, Antai, Aalu and others which have been detailed in Chapter I. All of these legends refer to a land sunk beneath the sea.

It is interesting to consider that, even today, certain of these races preserve traditions that they are descended from the Atlanteans or that their ancestors were culturally influenced by them. This is especially true of the Basques of northern Spain and southwestern France whose language has no connection with the other European languages. Traditions of a western continent are still held by the Berbers, whose language has certain points of similarity to Basque.

Belief in the existence of Atlantis is widespread...

a waterfall, ready for a dip. And then we headed out to Highway 11 and quickly realized that those with gutted homes were the lucky ones. For Highway 11 was just a couple of miles of pure destruction—crushed buildings, small apartment complexes wrecked, boats on the side of the road. One large trailer had one of those disturbing inflatable elongated demi-humans dancing grotesquely in the breeze outside it. It was an open business: Jack's Discount Cigarettes.

And as wrenching as this was, when you turned left just before the Highway 11 bridge, you could understand, finally, in all its stunning simplicity, what

happened here. You could see empty piles, those vertical logs, row after row of them on the lake. And if you didn't know what it meant, you'd pass them by, ascribing them to historical ruin. But those piles held fishing camps and houses that were simply gone. The sign remained for Vera's restaurant, which used to extend out to the lake and serve up awesomely crunchy and tender fried catfish. Across the road were boats pushed hundreds of yards ashore, piles of broken woods, a shambles. Nothing to look at, so we headed back to the bridge and on to St. Bernard Parish, feeling the aching mundanity of seeing ruin after ruin.

Chalmette:

If you had asked him, JB would have admitted that he was a goddamned idiot. A lucky goddamned idiot, but an idiot just the same. See, JB, a good friend of my brother, decided to stay behind when Hurricane Katrina struck the town of Chalmette, just across the line from New Orleans, in St. Bernard Parish. JB had himself a solo hurricane party, alone, gettin' drunk and thinkin' everything was gonna be just fine, as it had been with every other hurricane. "Then, I was standin' there in my underwear, holdin' a beer, and I noticed that the carpet was changin' color," he said, as his powers of perception told him that the flood after the storm was overtaking his small house close to Rocky and Carlos's seafood restaurant.

JB made a fateful decision at that moment, one that would make him put down the beer, one that would make him put on pants. He exited his house into the complete and utter darkness and water up to his waist. Imagine that for a moment here: There is no light, no glow of street lamps, no moon. Imagine being turned, in essence, nearly blind and then imagine being tossed into a river. JB got to his truck, which had one payment left on it. He tried the ignition. It turned over once and was dead.

The water rising, JB grabbed an ice chest that was floating by and he spent the next several hours in the water, "sometimes swimming, sometimes just lettin' the current take me along," the surging waters getting so deep that his feet couldn't reach the ground. Truth be told, JB, who's got a bum leg, nearly drowned many times over the course of that night, but he was a pigheaded son of a bitch, and the same stubborn attitude that made him stay in his home when so many others fled allowed him to continually recover and float on. Finally, he passed by a house that had a boat tied to the second floor window, the first floor by then underwater. The people there motored out into the water and rescued JB, bringing him back to their place. "But I was so tired, I just fell asleep in the boat. They put blankets on me and let me stay there."

The next day, the floods had receded enough so that JB could make his way to a crowded middle school serving as a shelter. Then began a bizarre odyssey through the "completely unprepared" so-called "emergency" system: To get food, JB headed out to the parish courthouse where, he said, "judges and politicians were havin' a big barbecue while handin' out peanut butter and jelly sandwiches to all of us." He was taken to a warehouse, jammed with people, poorly lit with only a few large box fans to keep the rescued cool in the ungodly Louisiana August heat. He was there for four days, "and I saw every kind of behavior—fights, people shootin' up drugs." There were few people of authority to control things. People were shitting and pissing everywhere, bargaining for food, buying drugs with food.

He was eventually removed to Algiers, across the river, and finally to the airport, where for a few more days he was warehoused. "They gave us one MRE and one bottle of water for every two people." The last part of his Louisiana journey was a fourteen-hour wait in a long line on the hot tarmac, without food or water, to be flown away to San Antonio, where he was taken in by a Baptist church until, a couple of weeks later, his family was able to bring him back to Lafayette, Louisiana. The church, which was housing a number of Katrina survivors, didn't want JB to go because "I had such a positive attitude, I guess they thought it had an effect on everyone else." But JB wanted to be with family since he was out of Chalmette, which, for all intents and purposes, didn't really exist.

We saw one working traffic light in all of St. Bernard Parish in late December 2005. There were checkpoints at every entrance to the parish, with police enforcing a dusk-to-dawn curfew since there was little or no power. The streets of Chalmette, of the whole parish, were ghostly still, with much the same ruin as the neighborhoods of Slidell. Except here there was no line where the destruction ended. It was all endless, endless. Outside of one faded old home was a Statue of Liberty lawn ornament, surrounded by debris. Another home was pushed into the middle of the street. And more, more trashed spaces.

Signs were posted all over the town—because, really, it was the only way to advertise—signs that offered the services of "House Gutters" and "We Tow Flooded Cars." The only visibly open businesses were liquor stores and some trailer operations, like "Shorty's Po-Boys," essentially a food truck, with a long line of customers wanting to get something other than Red Cross rations.

Which were readily available on the main street, Judge Perez Drive. You could see the death of a town on its empty main roads. For on Judge Perez, each and every business we passed was closed and/or gutted. Some of the parking lots of shopping centers were fenced off, creating large camps of FEMA trailers, with seemingly self-maintained checkpoints at the entrances. These would be crowded, traffic-filled roads and packed parking lots ordinarily. Chalmette's not a sleepy burg, but a bustling suburb. But then, four months after Katrina, it was a town of ghosts, living and dead.

JB died from cancer in April 2010. He never went back to his home in Chalmette. Kind of fucked up his entire adult life, he couldn't recover from the depression and despair he felt at the loss he experienced. No, that didn't give him cancer, but people who knew him, like my brother, say that it sure didn't give him the will to fight.

The Lower Ninth:

There's a good chance that there hadn't been this many white people in the Lower Ninth Ward of New Orleans since the last time the NOPD busted up a crack house. On that day, four months after the levee broke during Hurricane Katrina and sent a train roar of water heaving through the streets, the Ninth was crawling with white people in the neighborhood that fit CNN's Wolf Blitzer's definition of "so poor and so black." The white people crawled along in luxury cars to gawk at the destroyed community, nestled between very white Chalmette and, just on the other side of the Industrial Canal, the Bywater, a mixed-race community in New Orleans that gives way to the more gentrified Faubourg that gives way to the French Quarter.

Some white people got out of their cars to walk the shattered, muddy streets. Some took photos, most personal tokens, but some of them obviously for professional purposes. One young white man posed an older black man on a small stool, asking him to put his hands on his knees and lean forward.

The young white man wanted to take a picture of the older black man in front of the black man's collapsed house, dotted with his dirt-caked possessions. I hated that young white man. I wanted to kick his ass when he made the older black man re-pose. And then Gary reminded me that we ourselves were walking around, taking pictures, and, really, and, c'mon, were we that many steps removed from the photographer? My brother, a better angel, surely, if there is such a thing, said, "Isn't it better that people are coming to see this?" This, meaning, of course, everything around him.

To have entered the streets near the levee in the Lower Ninth Ward during that first year after the storm is to have witnessed the magnitude of the force of the floods. And it is to understand why the black people of the neighborhood believe they were abandoned. To put this in context: I visited the site of the fallen Twin Towers four months after 9/11. That was comprehensible horror—it was horror, to be sure, but it was concentrated, and we could grapple with that and understand it. We could see it all in a single wide-angle picture. Not the Lower Ninth Ward. Because one stationary camera would diminish the extent of the vast wasteland the neighborhood became, and the fact that virtually nothing had been done in the months since Katrina.

Herbert Gettridge was sitting on the porch of his stucco home, one of the few that remained standing without massive damage. Gettridge sat there as two other men were pulling out all of his belongings and tossing them into a pile. "I've been in this house for fifty years," he said, "raised nine children here. People know the Gettridges in the Lower Ninth." Yeah, he wanted everyone to know, the Lower Ninth Ward was poor and crime-ridden, but it was also a community of families and now the crime and families were gone, only leaving the poverty. He had rebuilt the house once before, after Hurricane Betsy in 1965: "I pulled out the old sheetrock by myself and put in all the new. I'll do it again." Of course, Gettridge was now eighty-two years old. "I just came back here from Madison, Wisconsin. FEMA sent us to seven different places, all over." He finally ended up with a daughter in Madison, with his wife, "been with the same woman since I was sixteen." His wife's sick, he said. "She wasn't doing too well before the storm and now she's feelin' worse." She remained in Madison.

The Gettridges had evacuated early, but so many others stayed behind or just couldn't leave. The attic of the house next door had a neat square hole cut in it. Gettridge's neighbor had stayed behind. "I told him he was a fool. Was in that attic for four or five days before the helicopter came and cut him out, half dead, no food or water." Another man across the street "lost his mind" because he stayed during the flood.

Gettridge's house was surrounded by the rubble and ruin of other houses. Most of the homes were knocked off their foundations by the rush and churn of the water from the Industrial Canal. Many were simply crushed—nothing but wood, insulation, roofing. A few were roofs on the ground with no house there. Cars were trapped underneath homes. Houses were split open like walnuts, cracked to reveal what was within, the belongings spilling out. And it essentially looked this way since the flood came. "Four months, and they haven't even moved the damn barge," Gettridge said.

Oh, yeah, the barge. There was a barge in the middle of the street next to the levee. Some believe the giant barge actually came unmoored in the storm and broke the levee. Some Lower Ninth residents say that they had complained about the barge before Katrina hit, that it was knocking against the levee earlier, and because it was Lower Ninth citizens, with no power at all, no one cared. But the barge was there that day, a huge rusting hulk. When it came through the levee, it smeared the houses right near it, like a gargantuan knife smoothing butter on a slice of toast. The water and barge shoved other houses

together into a jammed up pile. One of Gettridge's sons had a house in that pile. If the levee had held, yes, the neighborhood would still have been flooded, but it would have been more like Chalmette or Slidell, with houses turned into shells. Terrible enough, but not what it had become.

Walking near the barge, a large black man, about thirty years old, stepped out of a pickup truck and just started talking to us. "I've been in Oakland for the last three months. I just came back here today with my family. First time since I left on September 7." He hadn't been able to get out before the storm and he and his family rode it out before being taken to the I-10 overpass by someone with a small boat. "We were lucky because we had food and water up there. But it was horrible, man, horrible." He talked about shitting and pissing in front of other people, about old people dying around him. "I got two kids with me, six and ten, and they wanna know what's gonna happen. I wanna cry, but I can't cry, 'cause if they see their father cry, then they're gonna know everything ain't gonna be alright." He shook his head at the barge and walked away.

Back at Herbert Gettridge's house, we wished him luck and took his picture. I looked helplessly at my brother, who was speechless, too. Overcome with white liberal guilt, I handed him twenty bucks. "God bless you," Gettridge

said. "If I was still drinking, this would buy me two cases of beer." Gettridge said he'd given up drinking three or four years ago. If he had still been drinking, he'd have had an awfully long way to go to get a brew.

In Conclusion:

On New Year's weekend in New Orleans, Mid-City was dead. The ride down Carrollton in the center of the Crescent City was like going through an Old West ghost town—you half expected tumbleweeds and coyotes roaming the boarded up buildings and gray, dingy neighborhoods. Frankly, the city looks in many ways as it did in the late 1970s and early 1980s, when it was a sleazy, unruly Old South place, before the 1984 World's Fair, which, while it failed in so many ways, got the town gussied up and ready for guests. Of course, the sleazy streets, so often smelling of crushed magnolia, beer, and rainwater, were teeming with people then. It became the Big Empty. And just as the city will never be what it was in its stripper-and-rum era, it will never again be what it was before the storm.

In December 2005, other than the neighborhoods across the river, like Algiers and the Westbank, which got through Katrina relatively unscathed, all that really remained of New Orleans was a touristy mini-crescent north of the Mississippi River, encompassing the French Quarter, the Central Business District, and parts of the Garden District and Uptown. The resurrection of New Orleans seems as if it's calculated to create a Disneyfied version of itself, where only the parts that matter to outsiders are developed, those that can be made into simulacra of the real thing.

Re-creating what's been washed away is defeat, a desperate clinging to a past that Katrina wiped away. Goddamn, the Lower Ninth might have been a place of families and community and churches, but it was a poverty-stricken, forgotten corner that only surfaced in the collective consciousness of the city when there was violence. If the effort is made to keep the greedy sons of bitches away from the land there, something truly amazing can arise. But it won't. It hasn't. We are not that nation anymore, the one that has the will to do such things.

There's no climax here. No solutions. Just the New Orleans night, a darkness encroaching on the last bits of light.

Or maybe there is a personal denouement. After the trip, on the way back to Lafayette, Gary said he had been having doubts about Bush because he thought the war was useless. Now, having seen the wreckage of a place he loved, understanding that it didn't have to happen the way it did, "I think I'm giving up on Bush," he said. And he did. He bailed on knee-jerk conservatism. He bailed on Rush Limbaugh. All of it was worthless in the face of the real, physical effects of Republican failure.

In August 2010, one in four houses in New Orleans were still either wrecked or vacant. This is not the distant past. This is not a faraway place. This is here and this is now. ᴿᴾ

Slidell:

Much of Slidell has become a pretty close facsimile of what it was before Katrina. My brother and I rode through the same neighborhood where my friends' house was. >

Every sixth or seventh lot was either empty or contained a home that was still empty and ruined. In fact, my friend's place looked exactly the same as before, even though it had been sold pretty quickly. But the lawn was back. Otherwise, the neighborhood and the city looked normal.

Except, of course, at the waterfront. Almost all the fishing camps and homes along the stretch on Lake Pontchartrain were still missing. And where there had been wreckage there was now overgrown weeds. Freely growing weeds would prove to be something of a rule in the post-storm landscape.

Chalmette:

While most of Chalmette wasn't pretty pre-hurricane, it was a solidly mostly working class mostly white town. Now, the whole place just looks depressed, like it just got rundown and run over. Yeah, we ate at a packed Rocky and Carlos's, the great local Creole joint, but that says more about the resiliency of the oil industry than the entire economy there. On the main drag, we kept seeing closed businesses and empty lots, all up for sale. It was hard to tell, though, if that was all a result of Katrina, the BP oil spill, or the recession, or just some terrible gang bang by all three.

The Lower Ninth:

As we approached the Lower Ninth Ward again from the east, we were immediately plunged into a different realm of "recovery." We passed by boarded-up houses on the main drag of Claiborne Street, homes where the windows were broken, where the grass had grown up and over door frames, where the painted symbols of the rescue workers who had searched for corpses remained. "What the fuck?" I exclaimed. My brother couldn't answer. "Let's go see the where Brad Pitt's building houses."

Right near the rebuilt levee are a handful of small buildings that look like they are turds shat out of Frank Gehry's larger works. Brightly-colored houses with strangely angled and decorated walls and roofs among the empty lots and remaining devastation made it so that one block looked as if it was *The Jetsons* set in Bedrock. I mean, they're awesome-looking and free and green and shit,

and, hey, more power to Pitt for actually doing something. But I wondered what an old woman who had lived in the same ramshackle wooden house for 50 years would make of them. I still wondered if there wasn't some kind of unconscious hipster cultural colonialism going on.

We drove across the street from the Make It Right Pittville. We were instantly between two lots that were nothing but a jungle of weeds, as if we were lost on some backwoods rural road, not in the middle of a metropolitan area.

And then, as we went around the corner, we saw the rotting carcass of dog that had probably been there a while, judging from the way the skin on the head was curling away from the teeth.

My brother was tensing up. "I don't know what to say. I feel like I did last time. I'm speechless," he offered.

I responded, "I didn't think it would be this bad." Like right after the storm, you can't really get the magnitude of the abandonment of this

neighborhood unless you are standing there, in the middle of a street, and, with the exception of an anomalous house every couple of blocks, you are viewing a real-life version of those Discovery Channel shows about life after humans. Large swaths of the Lower Ninth, where over 14,000 people once lived, were returning to nature.

I'm not overstating it. There were chickens roaming the street. In some spots, the weeds and vines were overtaking the structures. I walked up to one house that had bees flying around the doorway and looked inside. Plants were growing inside, pushing through the floorboards. This one didn't even have a sign on it that it was scheduled to be condemned. It was just waiting to rot into the ground.

If you ever doubted the ability of this nation to do anything great anymore, walk the Lower Ninth. As I said before, it was an awful place, rank with poverty and crime. It was an exemplar of social neglect. Now, it stands (barely) as a demonstration of our American paralysis, of our failure to even take care of ourselves. RP

IT TOOK KATRINA TO PROVE THAT LIBERALS WERE RIGHT ALL ALONG

THE ONLY TIME MOST OF AMERICA RECOGNIZES THAT POVERTY EXISTS IS WHEN RIOTS HAPPEN, and then the political divide is something along the spectrum of "Them negroes have no self-control" to "Rioting is bad and maybe the >

negroes ought to be helped." Yep, poverty exists for all races (and it rose to 14.3 percent by 2009),[1] but the black face of it is all many Americans ever see.

Every once in a while, though, something untinged (for the most part) by violence occurs that demonstrates the real, awful, degrading condition in which millions of Americans attempt to exist (and this is not even to address the horrible conditions for the migrant workers and illegals attempting to create some approximation of an American life). For urban and suburban Americans, poverty exists as "the projects" or the neighborhood to avoid. And in rural America, poverty exists as Brigadoon-like towns, except shitty and shack-filled, seemingly appearing and disappearing[2] (and this is not even to address the horrible conditions for Native Americans on reservations attempting to create some simulacrum of an American life). For the most part, though, poverty is colored black, a perception which is borne out not just by the images from New Orleans, but by the latest stats, which say that the poverty rate is 9.4 percent for whites and 25.8 percent for blacks (with Hispanics a close second at 25.3 percent).

So Hurricane Katrina happens, ripping the scab off the wound that is the desperate day-to-day life of millions in this America. Even then, mostly, the right wing of the nation offered the familiar, almost monotonous variations on "individual responsibility" and "self-control." Get educated, they whine, stop having babies, don't be hippin' and hoppin' to yer gangsta rap. Most frighteningly, congressional Republicans, who were the majority back in 2005, declared that they were going to take on the issue, and they did, but through their cutely named "Republican Poverty Alleviation Agenda," which sought to filter money to churches and other charitable organizations, 'cause everyone's gotta take a taste, rather than actually setting up programs to deal with, say, alleviating poverty.

Every time something like a Katrina occurs, most liberals, the ones with memories that haven't been destroyed by all of the pot that we smoke to stay sane, shake their heads in disgust, 'cause, fuck, we've been down this goddamned road before. If you try to housebreak a dog and that fucker keeps shitting and pissing in the house no matter how many times you bring it outside, at some point you have to think that the dog is either stupid or mean or both. Your choices are to live with a house stinking of dog shit or to put that dog outside for good or send it to the pound. Right now, Democrats are living with the stench, and it doesn't matter if they are the majority or the minority. They have for the

1 Fun fact: in 1993, the poverty rate was 15.1 percent. It fell throughout the Clinton era, to 11.8 percent, before starting to rise again in 2001.
2 I remember driving through small roads in East Tennessee and Western North Carolina, and these collections of rusted mobile homes and tin-roof shacks would just appear, all with furniture and shells of cars on their front lawns, outhouses visible, and not a mouth of teeth among the people living there. I'd turn a corner and it was like they weren't even there.

last three decades. And real liberals are waving their arms, saying, No, we're humans, we don't have to live like this.

See, liberals believe in a very simple proposition: a stitch in time. You remember that old aphorism for darning socks? "A stitch in time saves nine"? Republicans are fond of saying that liberals want to just "throw money at" some problem whenever a program is suggested. Of course, just like after the invasion of Iraq, after Katrina, Republicans threw money at the Gulf Coast like a drunken exchange student at a German whorehouse. They retreated like sewer rats from their oft-stated position and offered up billions of dollars in such a haphazard way that it made the disastrous, corrupt reconstruction of Iraq look like a model of efficiency. Much of the tens of billions of dollars went to reconstruction efforts (or, to be more precise, to George W. Bush–connected corporations that hired contractors who hired workers for the cheapest wages with no oversight and immunity from lawsuits). But a whole fuck of a lot went to support families who, if, say, education and housing and job programs had been available in the years prior to the storm, might not be in as dire straits as they were. In other words, a little federal money back then in the right programs might have meant a lot less now. Essentially, in New Orleans especially, an entire neglected infrastructure finally got the attention it had needed for a long, long time. And it only took a thousand dead people for that to happen.

Liberals knew this and have been saying it for years: You will reap what you've sown, man, and if you sow hate and resentment and despair, sure, the short-term is a disenfranchised population that stays out of the political process so Republicans can win and continue the cycle. But the long-term is a bitch, and that bitch is the post-Katrina South.

The Great Society programs of the 1960s were a start and a possible solution. Remember the Great Society? Here's Lyndon Johnson in his 1964 speech that laid this shit out: "There is the decay of the centers and the despoiling of the suburbs. There is not enough housing for our people or transportation for our traffic. Open land is vanishing and old landmarks are violated. Worst of all expansion is eroding the precious and time-honored values of community with neighbors and communion with nature. The loss of these values breeds loneliness and boredom and indifference.... In many places, classrooms are overcrowded and curricula are outdated. Most of our qualified teachers are underpaid, and many of our paid teachers are unqualified. So we must give every child a place to sit and a teacher to learn from. Poverty must not be a bar to learning, and learning must offer an escape from poverty." Man, over forty years later, and those exact same words could be spoken. Doomed to repeat, doomed to repeat.

And so was born the 1965 Elementary and Secondary Education Act, the creation of HUD, the Fair Housing Act, Medicare, Medicaid, and a great deal more, which contributed to a massive drop in poverty levels, from 22.2 percent to 12.6 percent. Conservatives were apoplectic at these programs, seeing in them communism and social engineering, and, as ever, believed that individual states ought to take care of these things. Said Ronald Reagan in 1966: "[We should not] unquestioningly follow those others who pass the problems along to the federal government, abdicating their personal and local responsibility. The trouble with that solution is that for every ounce of federal help we get, we surrender an ounce of personal freedom. The Great Society grows greater every day—greater in cost, greater in inefficiency and greater in waste." Although you know what's fuckin' hilarious? One of the most controversial of the Great Society programs had the poor in their communities offering up ideas of how to improve those communities. Conservatives hated giving up power to the people they couldn't control.

Of course, as Johnson learned, worthless wars always fuck up budget initiatives, and programs were never funded as well as they could have been if he had ceased the insanity overseas. Then, of course, Nixon sliced some of the domestic programs. Then, of course, Reagan slashed Great Society programs with the zeal of a bacon addict on a pig farm. Programs for low-income families lost 54 percent of their funding, subsidized housing went down 80.7 percent, job and training programs were gutted by 68.3 percent, and housing assistance for the elderly went down by 47 percent. And they never recovered. And no state has ever made up for the loss.

It's always a big damn knee-slapper whenever conservatives say that "we tried" this "liberal" program or that for those living in poverty and "it failed." You hear that so often that it's become conservative and moderate dogma. The problem? At best, many of those programs were cut and burned before their full effects could be felt. Clinton was little help.[3] And Bush II sought to gut the remaining Great Society programs. At this point, Barack Obama has made up some ground, with there at least being access to health insurance for the poor. But the answer to conservatives is "How about we try some of those old liberal notions?" It's a stitch in time. Try to end poverty before something like the Katrina South rears its poor, black head and bites you on the ass, costing you not only the money to help the poor, but all the medical attention your own ass is gonna need.

'Cause, you see, you can give a man a fish and feed him once. But if you teach a man to fish, well, ya gotta provide him with the teacher, the fishing pole, the means of gettin' to the river, someone to watch the kids while he's fishin', the energy to cook that trout, the tools to cook the fish with.... RP

3 Remember, children, Bill Clinton was not a liberal. He was a leader, a real president, but he was a moderate conservative all the way.

NUNS AND GUNS

OH, WHAT FUN WE HAD AT THE ANTI-DEATH PENALTY MARCH IN BATON ROUGE, Louisiana, that hot November day in 1988. Yes, sir, we were ready to march our asses off to save the asses of prisoners down at Angola State Penitentiary. We >

gathered with Sister Helen Prejean outside the enormous capitol building, where inside you can step right up, step right up and see, with your very own eyes, the incredible bullet holes in the marble where Carl Weiss gunned down the great Huey P. Long. Yes, sir, and some of those holes were from the bullets that took out the scoundrel Dr. Weiss. It was capital punishment, my friends, at the Capitol. Sometimes the miracle of life is a complete circle.

We were a mighty crowd of a hundred walking through the deserted downtown streets on a Saturday morning. I didn't bring a sign, but I brought my heart. True, the only people who witnessed our powerful promenade of justice were the few tourists who just wanted us to get out of the way so they could measure Huey Long's bullet holes with their fingers, but our stroll to the Centroplex signified that the state could no longer be held blameless for the sins of the criminal justice system. Or perhaps it signified that no one in Louisiana beyond a few college students and a nun had any interest in those on death row. Ah, well, revolutions have started with less.

We arrived in an open area in the center of the Centroplex, a convention center and auditorium; it was a park-like space of several connected buildings. Apparently, no one had informed our organizers that a monthly gun and knife show was going on inside at the same time. But the banner outside the convention hall told us that it was the biggest gun show in the South.

So there we were, massed on a small lawn, chanting, "Two, four, six, eight, no one should be killed by the state." All around us were people carrying shotguns, pistols, samurai swords. A big, round, bearded man in overalls and a hat with a Confederate flag on it, a guy whose look screamed, "Redneck stereotype here. Come watch me nail my sister," stood on a catwalk, long double-barreled shotgun strapped onto him, staring down as a group of LSU actors performed a crazy sketch about a Kafkaesque nightmare of imprisonment, and you could tell he was wondering which of us to shoot first. Hoo, boy, I kept one eyeball on the speakers and one eyeball on gun and knife owners.

Sister Helen, who had been sitting the entire time, enjoying the performances, applauding for the impassioned and uncowed protesters, finally got up and spoke. If you've seen or read *Dead Man Walking*, you know what she spoke about—her work with death row inmates at Angola. She's lively and engaging and funny and self-deprecating (and looks nothing like Susan Sarandon), but she is deeply outraged by the ludicrousness of our approach to punishment in the United States. And she spoke as much to the redneck on the catwalk as she did to we who were with her on the march. How often does one get a chance to preach to the unconverted? How often do the sinners and the saints just happen to end up in the same place at the same time? No, Jeaux T. Overalls didn't fall on his knees and repent, but for a few minutes he stood there and listened, like good Cajun Catholics were taught to do when a nun spoke, and maybe he heard something he had never heard before. Maybe he heard something that made him reconsider, even briefly, what he believed.[1]

About fifteen years later, I met Sister Helen at another speaking engagement. I asked her if she remembered that day. She said she did. "That was very scary," she exclaimed. I was shocked and said that I didn't sense that she was scared. "Well, you never show them that," she replied. ⓡ

---

1 For those who right now are saying, "How does he know what Jeaux was thinking?" or "I knew a guy who loved guns and dressed in overalls who was against the death penalty," I can only say, "Blow me. You know as well as I do what 999 out of 1000 of those dudes believe."

NUDE WITH WEAPON

I WAS STAYING THE NIGHT AT A GIRLFRIEND'S APARTMENT while we were still in college. The girlfriend used to insist that we sleep nude, always, no matter the season, no matter how many of her roommates and their friends were around, when we entered her room to sleep, our clothes came off. The apartment >

was in a shitty section of town, right next to a bar and behind a carwash. There were four apartments in the building, all with college girls in them. But school was over, and the roommates were gone for the Christmas break and so sleepin' bare-ass with my girlfriend sounded like an all-you-can-bone buffet to a twenty-two-year-old male.

Now, Charlene slept with a loaded gun under her bed. Her daddy had given it to her to keep her safe. Hell, we'd even gone shooting with him sometimes, jackin' that cock-shaped fucker at a target in the distance at the range. Daddy even made his own bullets because it saved money. Beautiful.

So it's about three in the morning and, since I never really sleep, I hear the screen door squeak and some scraping and the front door opening. But I don't hear the screen door slam shut. And the problem was that we had used the door chain. So to open that door, you had to have undone the indoor chain from the outside. Fuck. And I hear footsteps slowly moving down the hall. Now, there I am, buck naked in our back room. Because we were always naked, and once her roommates walked in on me, I made sure the bedroom door was locked. Which pissed off Charlene, since she wanted to be all open and shit to the world.

Now, my pants are across the room, and I hear the footsteps getting closer, so I reach under the bed, grab the .38 snub-nose, and wait. Standing there, not a stitch on, holding a gun with two hands, staring at a locked door, looking for all the world like an NRA fantasy for losers, and I hear a hand on the door knob, trying it once, twice. By this point, Charlene had actually awakened. She could sleep through a nuclear explosion and wake up to wonder where the hell everybody was. She gestures at me to give her the gun. I gesture, "Fuck you."

I yell, "Whoever you are, I have a gun." And then I hear footsteps running away. We don't hear the door slam, so I hand Charlene the gun to hold on the door while I put on my jeans, even though at this point my balls have turtled themselves inside my groin. I take the gun and tell Charlene to put something on. The choice now is whether to go all Magnum PI down the hallway, jumping into rooms with the gun pointed out, or to cower in the bedroom. After cowering for a little while, we hear the garbage truck outside. Charlene throws open the window and calls after the guy loading bags into the hopper. He radios the cops, who arrive shortly after and show us that the screen door had been propped open with a house plant. Of course it had.

I don't know who it was that came into Charlene's apartment that night. The only thing that was missing was her giant chopping knife.

I got a little paranoid after that about locking doors and shit. Charlene thanked me for being there and making sure she wasn't raped and murdered, and then she dumped me a month later. I had a small round of therapy to understand why this peace-loving aspiring hippie was ready to pull the trigger and blow a hole in anyone who opened the bedroom door. "There's a difference between pacifism and passivism," the psychologist told me.

I got over it and decided to live my life a little bit more cautiously, putting away the knives, little things.

Now, if I had been like the United States after 9/11, I'd've changed the rules of engagement, man. I'd've put ten locks on the door, demanded to know why the neighbors wanted to borrow a cup of sugar, strip-searched everyone who entered my home, asked to know what they were reading, who they last saw, what they talked about, and why, why do they wanna visit? I'd demand DNA samples, collecting their urine and hairs for a collection in case something happened again. I'd go monkeyfuck insane, if I were America. Which I'm not. So, like I said, I just lock my door. 'Cause it might happen again, but if I cower under the covers, wondering what every bump means, I lost, man, I lost. **RP**

I WASN'T LIVING IN LOUISIANA

when David Duke, the former grand wizard of the Ku Klux Klan, ran for governor and then Senate, getting a majority of the white vote each time. But I was visiting during his Senate campaign. I headed over to Acadian Village with my buddy Neil. Acadian Village is a re-creation of >

an old South Louisiana town, like Williamsburg or Old Richmondtown in Staten Island. Costumed actors walk around and pretend to be townfolk, except with regular baths, modern dentistry, and a strange compulsion to explain everything they're doing. Acadian Village is modeled on early-nineteenth-century architecture. Or, in other words, we went to see a white supremacist speak in a place that was in slavery-era drag.

It was summer, so it was about 850 degrees and 10,000 percent humidity outside, which made the heat index say it felt fucking hot. Duke spoke to a small group of white people in an area of covered picnic tables. Man, that racist bastard was in his element, talking in just barely disguised code, saying things like, "I'm just saying out here the things we've been saying in the back rooms for years," which, according to the political spin decoder ring, translates to something like, "Those niggers and spics are ruining the place for the rest of us."

I listened and watched and knew, fucking knew, that evil existed, that we were in its presence, and the worst part was that so, so many people were willing to simply go along with evil, agree with evil, become evil. There, in a dusty field on a July day in Louisiana, when the sky brings thunderstorms every afternoon and you can taste electricity in the air just before they arrive, that was the true, unadorned, nearly perfect evil—charming, confident, complete. When David Duke asked for money to support his candidacy, Neil and I walked away. I heard people behind me, handlers of Duke's, asking, "Where are you going?" And we didn't turn back.

Even when people called after me, "Sir, sir, where are you going?" Even when Neil realized, "Oh, shit, that's my cousin," about one of the people following us. Even when one of his mindless drones tried to shove some literature into my hand. I didn't say a word. For what do you say? What do you say? We were outnumbered. Probably outgunned. And while I wouldn't say there were skinheads there, there were certainly big guys with close cropped hair who were mighty irritated that I was leaving without donating money or even shaking hands with the man who wore a Nazi uniform to taunt blacks and Jews while he was at Louisiana State University.

The next day, Neil saw his cousin at a family barbecue in Duson. They did not speak to each other.

You see, you have to go to where evil is to know what it's truly like. You have to be willing to put your ass on the line and not just stay tucked away in your little liberal lives, only seeing the people you love and admire, getting patted on the head and told your beliefs are right and good. I've done that, too, and it's like going to church. But it's when you hang out with the devil worshippers, the places where people are throwing themselves on the ground and sacrificing puppies to mad gods, that you really learn to confront the faithful. RP

Please turn the page for the
Analysis of Possible Republican Presidential Candidate,
Louisiana Governor **BOBBY JINDAL**

ANALYSIS OF POSSIBLE REPUBLICAN
PRESIDENTIAL CANDIDATES (#11 *of* 11)

LOUISIANA GOVERNOR

Bobby Jindal

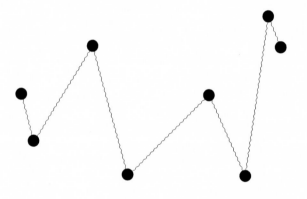

Dumbass

Distressingly
sinister

Downright
shameless

Discomfitingly
maniacal

Delightfully
weird

1971
1975
1990
1991
1992
1993
1994
1995
1996
1997
1998
1999
2000
2001
2002
2003
2004
2005
2006
2007
2008
2009
2010

1971: Born Piyush Amrit Jindal and, as soul-shredded research assistant Kristina noted, if they're gonna call the president "Barack Hussein Obama," then certainly Jindal's non-Bobby name will scare the yahoos.

1975: Gave himself the name "Bobby" because of the character of the same name on *The Brady Bunch*. Like his posture, it is pathetic, creepy, and endearing.

1994: Wrote an article where he talked about performing an exorcism with friends where they pinned a woman to the floor and prayed over her. Was kind of a pussy about it, too: "I began to think that the demon would only attack me if I tried to pray or fight back," so he stopped.

1997: Named secretary of the Louisiana Department of Health and Hospitals. Despite being praised by Rush Limbaugh, he apparently did some good things.

2004: Elected to Congress. Notable for being a non-white Republican who was fawned over like the sultan's favorite concubine, but accomplished little.

2007: Elected first Indian-American governor in the United States. Notable for being Indian-American and a governor.

2009: In a response to Barack Obama's state of the union address that was just pathetic and creepy, mocked "$140 million for something called 'volcano monitoring.'" Twisting the knife into science, Jindal added, "Instead of monitoring volcanoes, what Congress should be monitoring is the eruption of spending in Washington, DC." A month later, Mt. Redoubt in Alaska erupted, turning Jindal into a buffoon.

2010: After spending a year and a half talking about federal government interference in the states, begged for federal assistance as Louisiana was eaten alive by the BP oil blob.

☞ **PREDICTION**

Jindal says he won't run. He won't have a choice as a desperate GOP searches for someone of a different shade to go against Barack Obama. He'll lose when everyone realizes that Stephen Hawking has a stronger spine.

★
★
★
★
★
★
★

Part 7:
INTO THE WINTER

WORST FAMILY

IT'S RARE IN THIS WORLD WHEN YOU CAN GENERALIZE ABOUT AN ENTIRE FAMILY and not have to say, "with exceptions." For instance, you can talk about the immense and positive impact the Kennedys have had on the United States. But >

there's gotta be caveats, like Jack's war in Vietnam or William Kennedy Smith's date-raping ways. Perhaps it's just far, far easier to find evil families, where the lot of 'em are just a plague on their nations. Like maybe Saddam Hussein and his progeny. If, in around 2002, there had been some big Hussein family reunion and barbecue in Tikrit and everyone there had gotten poisoned by salmonella in the potato salad and died, not many people would have been terribly upset.

In the United States, you'd be hard pressed to find a family as comprehensively, actively odious as the Cheneys.[1] Indeed, there's not a single member of the Cheney family that the world would miss should they all be taken back to Hell, from whence they spawned, in one fell swoop.

Lynne Cheney

Mom Lynne has a Ph.D. in literature, having written a dissertation on one of the great dead white male poets, Matthew Arnold. Riding the anti-multiculturalism wave of the 1980s, Reagan appointed her the chair of the National Endowment for the Humanities, thus directly influencing a backlash against intellectuals that'd do Chairman Mao proud. And when Bill Clinton became president, she tried to get the NEH abolished. She published books about education where she whined about textbooks that consider "the architecture, labor systems, and agriculture of the Aztecs—but not their practice of human sacrifice."[2] She rode that post–Allan Bloom, anti-PC wave like a badass surfer bitch.[3] Before becoming second lady, she was a regular on cable news and a conservative think tank's wet dream. She was Coulter before Coulter was cool (which was just before Coulter stopped being cool). She writes insipid children's books that say things like, "F is for Freedom and the flag that we fly," "When the flag passes by in a parade, all persons should salute," oh, and, "G is for God in whom we trust," for mindless worship of America is what Lynne Cheney wants. Oh, yeah, and she sucks the cock of the man who said, "So?" about torturing people. She also allowed his penis in her vagina on at least two occasions, thus spawning his brood.

Liz Cheney

Constantly hoping for her Daddy's approval, Liz worked with her father to help choose a vice presidential candidate for George W. Bush, coming up at the end

1 The Bush family might count, but only for George H.W., Bar, and their kids. I just pity Laura, the twins aren't doing anything particularly evil, and George W. is presumably drinking mint juleps on the deck of his Dallas house while he dictates random shit to his ghostwriter.
2 For bonus points, she co-scrawled a novel about a fifty-nine-year-old Vice president who dislikes the president and dies of a heart attack. Her husband was fifty-nine when he became Vice. The book's publication date was 1998. Its name is oh-so-clever: *The Body Politic*.
3 A note here: Do you ever hear anyone complain about the number of conservatives in the financial industry? Or the oil industry? Or the insurance industry? Or the pharmaceutical industry? No, but when it comes to academia, all of a sudden they're all concerned about diversity of thought.

of the day with Dick. Daddy rewarded Liz for choosing him to be Vice by forcing Colin Powell to hire her for a position in Near Eastern Affairs. As a campaign hack in two elections, she defended her father and his "boss" like she was Cerberus at the gates of Hades. As the Cheney vice presidency was ending in 2008, Liz worked for both Fred Thompson and Mitt Romney, helping them both lose. Now, she inhabits a role as an advocate for her father's decadent view of the world, and, particularly on Fox "news," she has demonstrated a skill in hyperbole and hysterical theatrics that'd make Al Pacino at his scenery-chewing worst say, "Whoa, just calm the fuck down there." She thinks we should be at war with Iran, that Israel is more important than anything else, and that Barack Obama doesn't love the nation. Her organization, with the stupid-ass name of Keep America Safe, has provided a nonprofit way to lie to the Americans she wants to keep safe. Oh, Daddy, Daddy, dontcha love me now? Dontcha?

Mary Cheney
Lesbian Mary passed through Lynne's vaginal lips second, but during the two presidential elections, she was first in everyone's thoughts. When Lynne was asked about her "openly lesbian daughter," Mom blanched and reflexively denied it, even getting pissed about the question. But this didn't seem to bother Gay Mary, who was evolving into the most self-loathing conservadyke, or, in other words, a proud Republican. Mary worked for Coors, the proudly anti-gay, pro-life, anti-union, shitty-beer-making company. Her job? To get gays to drink the shitty beer. Supporting her father meant supporting George W. Bush, who spoke about the need for a constitutional amendment declaring that marriage is only between two very unlucky people of different sexes. Of the conundrum of getting paid by the Bush campaign, she said in her memoir, "I needed to know if I could work for the re-election of a president who wanted to write discrimination into the Constitution of the United States. It wasn't an easy decision for me to make, and in the days that followed I came very close to quitting my job as the director of VP operations for the Bush-Cheney '04 campaign. I seriously considered packing up my office and heading home to Colorado." But she didn't. She stayed by dear ol' Dad until she made sure that her equal rights would be denied for the next four years.

Dick Cheney
Let's just bottom-line this and not go through every single Beelzebub-approved thing Cheney has done, without talking about Halliburton and torture and energy task forces and all of that stuff you should know by now[4] (and if you don't,

4 No, really, you should know about the vast majority of the Pinochet-like crimes and appalling statements of the former vice president.

then you should probably get up to speed on twenty-first century history): There are American citizens who are actually, diabolically evil. And I'm not talking about the occasional failed terrorist or pathetic white loser who hopes to find friends in jihad over in Pakistan. No, there's villains in the old mold, the vile industrialists and politicians. Dick Cheney is a villain. He wishes to do harm. He does not care who gets hurt, as long as he and his friends profit. And he has a monarchical attitude toward the government that he contorts the Constitution toward in order to justify it and not seem like the murderous, treasonous, covetous cretin he actually is.

But, hey, if you're looking for further proof, here ya go:

In 1986, regarding the weapons the United States, through the CIA, was sending to the "rebels" in Afghanistan who were then engaged in their years-long war with the Soviet Union, the *New York Times* reported that then-Representative Richard Cheney of Wyoming "believes American interests are likely to be increasingly tied to support of anti-Soviet forces in the third world."

On February 4, 1988, on the *MacNeil/Lehrer Newshour*, talking about the "rebels" driving back the Soviet Union, Representative Cheney said, "A key point on Afghanistan and the Afghan move: the Mujahideen have stopped Soviet aggression dead in its tracks, and the Soviets are talking about withdrawing. But we sent them one hell of a lot more than boots and bandages to get that done."

In 1990, when he was George Bush the Smarter's secretary of defense, Cheney was an advocate for the policy of arming the "rebels" in Afghanistan. Also financing and arming the mujahideen was a Saudi from a wealthy family, Osama bin Laden, who got fighters from mosques around the globe. So Dick Cheney and bin Laden once, more or less, worked together. After the war with Afghanistan helped to destroy the Soviet Union, various mujahideen groups became the Taliban and Al Qaeda.

In other words, Dick Cheney's actions led directly to 9/11.[5]

The fact that Cheney is a free man, decaying from his desiccated heart to his gout-ridden legs in his huge houses paid for by oil profits, speaks of just how feckless and corrupted our body politic has become.

CONCLUSION

Picture Dick and Lynne balling madly on a horsehide sofa, the rough bristles just making them crazier. They both hold remote controls in their hands, Dick has one to adjust the speed of the small vibrator in Lynne's asshole while hers can speed up or slow down Dick's pacemaker. They tumble off the sofa and onto a rug that's a patchwork image of the fifty states. Fucking across the Plains, staining the Gulf Coast, drooling on the Northeast, cumming on DC, defiling the entirety of the nation. ⟨RP⟩

5 And this has nothing to do with the whole "9/11 truth" movement. Remember: no conspiracy theories allowed.

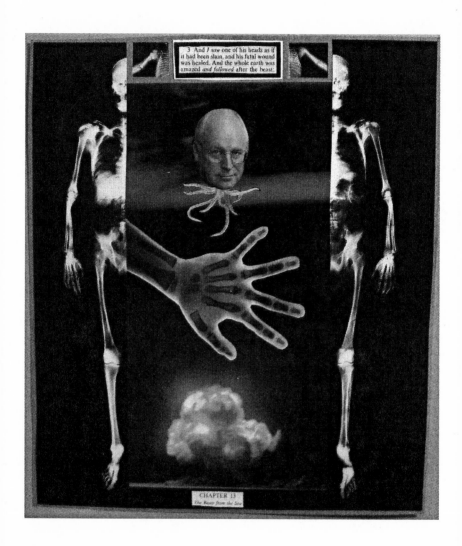

Cheney in Repose: A poem

(A merging of former Vice President Dick Cheney's February 4, 2009,
 interview with reporters from *Politico* and actor Christian Bale's on-set
explosion at a director of photography during the filming of *Terminator
3: Rise of the Machines*.)

These are evil people. And we're not
going to win this fight by turning the other cheek.
You're unbelievable man, you're un-fucking-believable.
No, don't just be sorry, think for one fucking second.
What the fuck are you doing? Are you professional or not?
The United States needs to be not so much loved
as it needs to be respected. Sometimes,
that requires us to take actions that generate controversy.
I'm not at all sure that that's what the Obama
administration believes. What the fuck is it with you?
What don't you fucking understand? You got any fucking idea about
the ultimate threat to the country?
A nuclear weapon or a biological agent of some kind?
That's the one that would involve the deaths of perhaps hundreds
of thousands of people, and the one you have to spend
a hell of a lot of time guarding against. You don't fucking
understand what it's like. That's what that is.
It's unlike anything I've ever seen. The combination
of the financial crisis that started last year, coupled now with,
obviously, a major recession,
I think we're a long way from having solved
these problems. Let's go again. Let's not take
a fucking minute; let's go again.

>

When we get people who are more concerned
about reading the rights to an Al Qaeda terrorist
than they are with protecting the United States against
people who are absolutely committed to do anything they can
to kill Americans, then I worry. Somebody should be fucking
watching and keeping an eye on him. I'm fucking serious.
You're a nice guy. You're a nice guy, but that don't fucking cut it
when you're bullshitting and fucking around like this.
If you release the hard-core Al Qaeda terrorists that are
held at Guantánamo, I think they go back into
the business of trying to kill more Americans and
mount further mass-casualty attacks. I'm not asking you,
I'm telling you. You wouldn't have done that otherwise.
If you turn 'em loose and they go kill more
Americans, who's responsible for that?
Gimme a fucking answer. What don't you get about it?
Fuck's sake, man, you're amateur.
I think there's a high probability of such an attempt.
Whether or not they can pull it off depends on
whether or not we keep in place policies that have
allowed us to defeat all further attempts,
since 9/11,
to launch mass-casualty attacks against the United
States. Well, somebody should be watching him
and keeping an eye on him. He doesn't give a fuck
about what is going on.

>

I'm gonna fucking kick your fucking ass
if you don't shut up for a second, alright?
If it hadn't been for what we did, with respect to
the terrorist surveillance program, or enhanced
interrogation techniques for high-value detainees,
the Patriot Act, and so forth
then we would have been
attacked again. What is he doing
there? Do you understand?
You've got something to say to this prick?
Seriously man, you and me, we're fucking done.
Fucking ass.

I think there are some who probably
actually believe that if we just go talk
nice to these folks, everything's going to be
okay. Do you want me to fucking trash them?
Those policies we put in place,
in my opinion,
were absolutely crucial to getting us through
the last seven-plus years without a major-casualty
attack on the U.S.
And how was it?
I hope it was fucking good,
because it's useless now,
isn't it?

GLENN BECK
IS THE NEW
MARTIN LUTHER KING
(IN HELL)

GLENN BECK, January 15, 2010, on race in America:
> "We're really taking a—really taking our direction from
> Martin Luther King."

GLENN BECK, March 24, 2010, on welfare programs:
> "Voluntary charity doesn't go far enough? Give to the poor
> by taking from the rich? Unfortunately that means theft."

MARTIN LUTHER KING, JR., in "The Domestic Impact of the War,"
a speech delivered on November 11, 1967, to the National Labor
Leadership Assembly for Peace:
> "In the past two months unemployment has increased
> approximately 15 percent. At this moment tens of
> thousands of people and anti-poverty programs are
> being abruptly thrown out of jobs and training programs
> to search in a diminishing job market for work and survival.
> It is disgraceful that a Congress that can vote upwards of
> $35 billion a year for a senseless immoral war in Vietnam
> cannot vote a weak $2 billion dollars to carry on our all-
> too-feeble efforts to bind up the wound of our nation's 35
> million poor. This is nothing short of a Congress engaging
> in political guerrilla warfare against the defenseless poor of
> our nation."

**THE CHRISTMAS SWEATER
THAT STOLE CHRISTMAS**

I WOULD RATHER HAVE MY BALLS WAXED BY A BEAUTICIAN WITH HOOKS FOR HANDS than have to sit through Glenn Beck's performance of *The Christmas Sweater* again. While recognizing that Beck's daily ear and eye mauling on radio >

and TV certainly have an effect on my perception, I can say that, based on everything I've seen of or read by the man, Glenn Beck is one of the most despicable human beings on the earth who does not have the power to decide life or death. A truly just God would have buried him up to his neck in dense shit and then sent a plague of flies to lay eggs in his head.

Which, come to think of it, is not unlike watching *The Christmas Sweater*. This is not merely a response to Glenn Beck or his "politics" (the quotation marks will be explained later); I must see at least 100 plays and performance pieces a year, as well as having done my own one-person show thing (and, you know, having a Ph.D. in this shit). But let's not get ahead of ourselves.

The idea of *The Christmas Sweater*, as promulgated by Beck, is that the conservative talk show host and "media giant," as his promotional video modestly calls him (he'd say it was a joke, you can be sure), is going to reveal "my greatest shame." Instead, what Beck did was write a novel about a young boy and said sweater. That led Beck to create and act and tour in an elaborate one-man show, with a small orchestra, video images, and the obligatory large black woman singer, one performance of which was simulcast and "rebroad-cast" several times to movie theaters around the country during Christmas 2008, which leads to Christmas season 2009, when Beck staged *The Christmas Sweater: A Return to Redemption* at the Skirball Center in New York before a live audience, with simulcast at movie theaters around the country.

Here's what Beck promised for the show: "Before a live audience, Glenn will tell you about the real life events that inspired him to write *The Christmas Sweater*, and he'll share stories of the overwhelming response he received about how the tale's message of redemption literally changed people's lives, bringing many back from the brink of collapse and restoring family relation-ships. Then, Glenn will show a brand new, re-mastered and exclusive version of *The Christmas Sweater* taped live during his 2008 cross-country tour. Afterward, Glenn will introduce you to some of the people who were touched by the story, and through inimitable interviewing style you'll experience their intimate journey of transformation through the simple gift of redemption."

The show itself started fifteen minutes early, with Beck talking to us in that passive-aggressive, aw-shucks, fuck-you-wanna-punch-him-in-his-pudgy-face voice of his, about how great his story is and how the economy sucks. Then we get a few minutes of carols sung by a second-tier black choir (apparently, in Beck's world, only black people can sing Christmas songs), the first hav-ing bailed on him when someone pointed out that they'd be singing for Glenn

Beck. After a brief, teary intro by the man himself, revealing that one year he had to buy Christmas gifts for his kids at CVS and gesturing to some very uncomfortable-looking people sitting on the stage, he tells us we're gonna watch the video from last year. It should be mentioned here that this cost twenty bucks just to sit in the movie theater. And it wasn't even in 3-D. Actually, that should read, "Gratifyingly, it wasn't in 3-D."

Here's the short version of the story: A twelve-year-old boy named Eddie lives in some ridiculous parody of an idyllic Americana town right out of the Disney garbage bin. Eddie's dad is dead, his mom works a couple of jobs, and it's Christmastime. Eddie wants a bike, Mom gives him a sweater she made, Eddie throws it in a corner, Mom is sad, they drive to Grandma and Grandpa's farm, Eddie's a dick the whole time, they leave early, they get into a head-on collision, Mom dies, Eddie ends up living with the grandparents, he meets a mysterious filthy old ranch hand named Russell who wants him to accept that shit happens, Eddie's prick grandpa shows him the bike he would have gotten if he hadn't been such a douchebag, Eddie steals the bike and runs away, he crashes in a corn field, he curses Jesus, he sees a giant storm heading his way, he's scared, creepy Russell walks out of the cornfield to get Eddie to walk into the storm, Eddie does it, he ends up in a field of flowers, it turns out Russell's God or Jesus or something, Russell-God-Jesus-or-Something tells Eddie he has to face his storms, Russell disappears into light, Eddie wakes up in bed on Christmas morning with his mom still alive and he gets a re-do of the day. There is much weeping.

Beck's performance involves lots of throwing himself on the floor, rolling around, doing stereotyped voices for every character, and crying, until at some point it becomes a parody of crying. That would probably be when Beck is fetal on the ground, sobbing while the fat black woman sings something. Oh, and he uses a teleprompter.

The script itself[1] is so vilely calculating, conceived to parade every possible cliché in front of us, that, if Beck were a smarter man, it might seem like some Andy Kaufmanesque prank that mocks the audience for believing there actually was an America in the 1970s, when this takes place, where kids rode red bikes and said, "For Pete's sake" and "Golly" and "This is the bestest Christmas ever" (that's not a joke). It's like he took every overused Christmas story element short of a Grinch, tossed it into a blender, beat Jimmy Stewart's zombie corpse back in when it tried to climb out, and then threw in a bleeding Jesus doll.

1 And the book, which I read while vomiting nonstop with a stomach ailment and figured why not kill two birds with one virus.

The Christmas shit is fine, bland, whatever. But when the story gets into redemption mode? That's when it goes bugnuts. Beck's image of the swirling storm that represents life's challenges and the urgings of Russell are the stuff of sub–Joel Osteen hope-mongering. And it left me wondering, "What's that skeevy fucker up to?" Beck's put himself into the role of motivational speaker, about how once you face the storm in your life, you can heal or some such shit. Fuck him.

But, mostly, Beck is a fucking liar, a con artist, and a sociopath. After the video of his sweaty, slobbering, sobbing performance, Beck cries and tells us that his publisher made him change the ending to have Mom come back to life. How do I know Beck is lying? If all that choking up and crying is real, this fucker is dangerous to himself and others. Besides, he's got a fucking tell: his pause just before each time his throat catches. It's consistent and exactly the same each time. No one cries the same way every time.

But that's not the worst of it. Put aside for a moment that the entire enterprise was a two-and-a-half-hour infomercial to make us buy his goddamn book. The lies just start to pile up. Beck told us he was going to reveal the truth behind the story. But he doesn't. He teases us with the notion that "elements" of it are true so that people watching it conflate his story with Eddie's. But that's another lie, a lie he doesn't dispel at all. He's not Eddie, his mom didn't die on Christmas; his parents got divorced in Beck's real life—death is less messy than divorce, no?—but Beck is consciously tricking his audience into believing a story that is as much a fantasy as *It's a Wonderful Life*. Beck's redemption wasn't an overnight transformation in a cornfield when he was twelve. It was actually years of work to overcome alcoholism to be the dry-drunk, hateful maniac he is today.

And nothing is below him in his attempt to ennoble his fucking lie of a story. Here's the worst part (yes, there is a worst part): The last segment of the evening was Beck showing us videos of the stories of people he says were "inspired" to face their "storms" by reading *The Christmas Sweater* or hearing Beck's voice. No, really, one guy said he was heading into a drug store to get sleeping pills to off himself; then he heard Beck speaking, and it caused him to fall to the street sobbing and not kill himself (although being a drama queen in public is fine). The other people Beck "saved" are a former heroin addict (who says he got serious about doing drugs on 9/11), a breast cancer survivor, and the aforementioned suicidal guy. Their stories are highlighted with quotes from the book about, you know, facing storms. They were brought out to a couch to vouch for the greatness of Beck and the sweater. Each of them said they're glad they suffered, glad they were addicted to drugs, glad they had breast cancer, because of what it taught them about life. Whether or not such lessons might have happened minus a mastectomy are never part of this equation.

But the fucking con job is completed in a sloppy way. For there's one other woman. She is there to illustrate getting past loss. See, one Christmas Day, she, her husband, and their three-year-old daughter were riding to the grandparents' house when they got in a collision with another car, killing the husband and little girl. The woman went through a long recovery, but she decided to live her life to the fullest, doing things her little girl loved, like learning to ride horses, and she devotes her life to rescued dogs. It's actually quite a lovely tale. What does Beck's book have to do with it?

Fucking nothing. The accident happened in 1986, while Glenn Beck was a nobody jerk-off DJ, and Beck had nothing to do with the woman's "redemption." In other words, Beck was looking for someone who had lost someone in a car accident on Christmas Day just like Eddie in order to illustrate some fucking point in his awful story. In other words, it's a lie to prop up his other lies.

That cynicism, that utter contempt for humanity and suffering, that ability to freely exploit the awful events of others, that is what Beck does. Whether it's about God, the nation, or your pain. In more than a few ways, his big ass rally on August 28, 2010 in DC was merely *The Christmas Sweater* in bigger, bolder, letters.

The word "politics" is in quotation marks above because there are no real political foundations behind Beck's beliefs. He spouts a vague, nebulous form of nationalism without grounding it in any real-world policy (except a complete set of lies about what the founders wrote). It is governance-lite; or, more accurately, it is anarchy. His religious beliefs, as exemplified by the fictional story of Eddie, are devoid of actual Christian suffering and redemption. It's faith without much more work than a good therapy session. In other words, he has no beliefs at all, other than to suck your wallets dry, but he disguises that fact in words, words, words and tears, tears, tears.

On February 17, 2010, a few months after writing the blog version of this story, I received an email from JoZ:[2]

> I am the woman on Glenn Beck's couch that lost her 3 yr. old
> daughter, Leslie, when a woman fell asleep in her car and plowed

2 I've cleaned up much of JoZ's grammar (although I left the exclamation marks since she wanted to convey her enthusiasm. And I've left her name out of here on purpose).

into mine. I have had many people send me reviews. Most people say kind things. Most people comment on the other people on the couch. Some people have said, 'Why was I there?' or 'They could have done an entire show on my life and it would have been more interesting!'

Besides the fact that F**K seems to be an OK word to use nowadays, although my mother always taught me that people who use curse words are of the lower class because they don't take the time to use proper words, I did actually make it through the entire write-up that you wrote. Sigh!!

Anyhow, the only reason I agreed to do the show was because IF there were one person who was out there in a movie theater who was on the edge regarding their own lives—so many things had happened to them that they couldn't take another step—I hoped they would take my story and think maybe they can take that other step to live and do something with their lives!!

Many people I have come into contact with since the accident happened back in 1986 don't really know what happened because, if you tell someone that your only child died, they run away as fast as they can. I mean, really, how do you explain that?? They either over-react or say they understand, which they don't!!

Glenn's show was to show all sorts of people, some of whom fell upon their own swords (doing drugs, needles, whatever) and some people who had crap dumped on them, like me and the lovely young lady with cancer, that we all can weather the storms in our lives, even if it is one step at a time !!!

I feel badly for the people who just couldn't get past Glenn Beck's persona.

There are some people who see the glass as half empty (pessimists), and then there are the people who see the glass as half full (optimists), and then there are the people who barely have a glass to hold.

Which one are you?? I think that people who can only find the snarky nasty ways of talking about people are truly talking about themselves!!

Have a great life.

JoZ, #1 Couch Person

Glenn Beck's *The Christmas Sweater: A Return to Redemption*

And I responded:

Dear JoZ,

Thanks for writing to me. Your life story is compelling and moving, and you'd obviously have to put me firmly in the group who would have rather listened to you speak than Beck. If you haven't yet written a book, you should. You offer a real tale of reassurance and redemption in the face of one of the worst tragedies imaginable. I understand your desire to reach out to people.

I'm sure that the other guests on stage with you are perfectly nice people who have suffered and learned through their suffering, even if I might disagree with the notion that people are glad they went through the awful things they have been through. I think that's something we tell ourselves to make sense of the terrible in our lives.

However, my issue was not with you. It was with Glenn Beck and his manipulation of you and the others in order to sell books. I don't know if you saw a recording of the show, but it was essentially a long infomercial for Beck and his books. Each of your segments was introduced as highlighting something Beck wrote in *The Christmas Sweater*, and those of you on stage there were offered as examples of how people were affected by the book.

To do so with your story, when you had so obviously learned how to live your life without his help, was, at best, deliberately misleading. While you may have had good reasons for being there, ultimately Beck was crassly exploiting you. The entire event was framed by ads for the book.

This all has little to do with my optimism or pessimism. Actually, since you asked, I am quite an optimistic person. It's why I despise Glenn Beck. He traffics in doom and fear when he's not peddling a bastardized version of Christian redemption. I think that Beck is doing more to damage people's lives in general. And his attempts at self-help proselytizing strike me as the con game of a huckster.

I think what he did was shameful. You have far more to offer the world than Glenn Beck ever will.

Be well, and, truly, my best to you.

I then got a much longer letter from JoZ about the behind-the-scenes at the Beck show (which is excerpted here):

Hello again Lee,

When I saw your e-mail come in, I wasn't too sure if I could take another snarky bunch of comments, but I was definitely surprised by your response.[3]

The whole thing with Glenn Beck was definitely interesting, and even though I did understand that not only was he promoting his book, he was trying to help some people, if not himself. Like I said before, I was only interested in letting people know out there that crap happens, sometimes BIGTIME like me, and sometimes in small ways. But not too many people I know get through life without any scars. Some people have them on the outside. Some on the inside! I am just one 'little' person who doesn't have access to any sort of large TV or movie audience, so being on a Christmas show (which, by the way, was Leslie's favorite time of year and, since her death, the worst time of year for me) and for some reason when I sent in my story, it didn't take the producers too long to get a hold of me and ask if I would be part of the show. When the production company came down to my house in PA, I thought they were coming with one little camera and a person. I was shocked when the whole production company showed up, limos and all.

When the show's producers interviewed me, Arlene, and my Dad, for 3–4 hours (don't forget Sarah, my rescued Scottie), I made sure to get across certain points: animal rescue, therapy for handicapped people on horseback, faith, hope, and love for many people who didn't know what to do when Leslie died and avoided me and such. I asked them how my story would fit in with Glenn's current book since all of this happened 20 years ago and I was raised in a family of people who do not brag about themselves and their accomplishments. The producers understood what I was saying, but even though the book came out later than my accident and following

3 I'm pretty sure she expected some drunk monster at a keyboard, laughing madly at her pain, shooting up heroin while humping tattooed and pierced whores. But that's Friday. I wrote to her on a Thursday.

endeavors, my case would show people that there are large storms, small storms. Eddie's storm was self-inflicted by his hatred of the situation he found himself in, and the longer he stayed in the hateful, angry place the longer his storm lasted.

JoZ went into detail about her life story. Let's allow that to be private. She continued:

> Oh, I did get to see the show on the reprise night. I watched it through my fingers as if they would shield me from the purple blouse that was chosen for me. I was more worried about falling off the couch since my rheumatoid arthritis was really hurting and there weren't any more pain meds I could take. I didn't smile either (which is so not me) because somehow I thought I would talk too much about my story and the other people wouldn't be able to talk. I worried about sitting up straight. I worried about not falling off the couch (notice I mention that twice lolol). I was really interested in all the goings-on behind the scenes: The production part was really cool, fascinating stuff. I wasn't nervous about being on the stage, just falling off of it since it was a live show lolol. But all in all I think my story came across a bit because while leaving the movie theater, I had 4–5 people come up and tell me their stories and that they were glad to see we should have hope even in today's world.

There's no big ending here. JoZ and I didn't become pen pals or e-mail buddies. We never celebrated a holiday together. She believed what she did was good. It might have been for some people. Glenn Beck crassly sold books. Both of these things are possible at once. 🅟

IMAGINE THOMAS PAINE.
It is the humid, fetid
summer of 1794 in
Luxembourg Prison in
Paris. Imagine Thomas
Paine in a cell in that
prison in a former
palace. He has by this
time in his life written
Common Sense and >

The American Crisis papers, works that George Washington read aloud to his troops to give them the courage to fight on. He had been given a farm in New Rochelle, New York, to thank him for his contribution to the "cause of independence" in America. He is known by all of them: Washington, Franklin, Jefferson. He could have retired to his farm. He does not. He could have merely worked for the new government. He does not. It isn't exciting enough. Thomas Paine is an inventor, after all. If he can't create a smokeless candle or design an iron bridge, then he must invent nations and political systems.

So he is in France, moving from one revolution to another. Having written *The Rights of Man*, which said that all men should be involved in determining how government is run, not just an aristocracy or royalty, having been given French citizenship and elected as a delegate to the National Convention, having been one of the writers of France's new constitution, he now finds himself in jail, awaiting the guillotine, which could come at any time. Scores of prisoners a day are so killed. His crime? He wanted King Louis XVI to be banished, not executed. In fact, he wanted capital punishment outlawed. This was a bad move in a nation enamored of beheadings. For the treason of wanting the king to live in exile, he was arrested on December 28, 1793.

The founders of America were not costume characters. They were not animatronic dolls at a Disney World ride. No, they were flesh and blood humans who, when they opposed the British, risked hanging, as well as having every bit of property taken from their families. Today, when members of some movement or other say that they are new revolutionaries because they want to cut taxes or oppose a national health care system, they inevitably compare themselves to the founders. Those people need to be asked if they would be part of, say, the Tea Party movement if the end result of losing might be getting captured and hanged and having their houses burned to the ground.
They need to be told to imagine Thomas Paine. The real Thomas Paine, not the fantasy Paine conjured by those who would deny how genuinely revolutionary and liberal he was.

They need to know that in *American Crisis V*, he wrote, "If there is a sin superior to every other, it is that of willful and offensive war. Most other sins are circumscribed within narrow limits, that is, the power of one man cannot give them a very general extension, and many kinds of sins have only a mental existence from which no infection arises; but he who is the author of a war, lets loose the whole contagion of hell, and opens a vein that bleeds a nation to death."

They need to know that, in *The Rights of Man*, he wrote, "Hunger is not among the postponable wants, and a day, even a few hours, in such a condition is often the crisis of a life of ruin." And that Paine had very specific plans for using tax money to hire impoverished people: "To erect two or more buildings, or take some already erected, capable of containing at least six thousand persons, and to have in each of these places as many kinds of employment as can be contrived, so that every person who shall come may find something which he or she can do." And that Paine wanted to provide welfare from tax revenue so that "[t]he hearts of the humane will not be shocked by ragged and hungry children, and persons of seventy and eighty years of age, begging for bread. The dying poor will not be dragged from place to place to breathe their last, as a reprisal of parish upon parish. Widows will have a maintenance for their children, and not be carted away, on the death of their husbands, like culprits and criminals; and children will no longer be considered as increasing the distresses of their parents." That was written over half a century before Marx, but it is surely far more socialistic than any program the United States has ever implemented. But mostly they need to imagine Thomas Paine in that cell in 1794 in Paris. Imagine him in the present tense, not the past. He can hear the crowds gathered at the guillotine. He is suffering from a fever that the French summer and the cramped space have brought on. He feels abandoned by the American leadership, his entreaties to Washington ignored. Some, like Gouverneur Morris, even wish he would be executed. And he is writing a new book, *The Age of Reason*.

If previously Paine sought to undermine the legitimacy of monarchy, now he is going after what he sees as the other hindrance to actual democracy flourishing: organized religion. In the introduction of *The Age of Reason*, scrawled while living in that cell with the sounds of his own doom echoing around, Paine writes, "I do not believe in the creed professed by the Jewish church, by the Roman church, by the Greek church, by the Turkish church, by the Protestant church, nor by any church that I know of. My own mind is my own church. All national institutions of churches, whether Jewish, Christian, or Turkish, appear to me no other than human inventions set up to terrify and enslave mankind, and monopolize power and profit. I do not mean by this declaration to condemn those who believe otherwise; they have the same right to their belief as I have to mine." Paine fears "the adulterous connection of church and state," and he believes that "a revolution in religion" can happen. He affirms his own belief in God, but he spends the rest of the book tearing apart the Bible and asserting that God doesn't bother with the affairs of humans. It is an angry book by an angry man.

Paine will be freed in November 1794, after entreaties from James Monroe finally work and the bloodlust in France is ending. He will not return home yet. Instead, he will go back to the National Convention to finish the work he started. He will publish *The Age of Reason*. He will come back to the United States in financial ruin in 1802, by invitation of Thomas Jefferson. He will return to a nation beginning to be gripped by a mad religious revival known as the Second Great Awakening. He will be branded an atheist and a disgrace. Despite help from Jefferson, he will become political poison to other founders. He will die alone in New York City, a broke alcoholic in 1809.

Ask people who believe they know Thomas Paine if they could have done what he did. Ask them if that's how much they have faith in the importance of their cause. Ask them if they could have spent nearly a year in prison with their door marked for execution. They could not. They won't ever have to because Paine did it for them already, no matter what they believe. ⬤

CONCLUSION

The day Ronald Reagan was shot, I was in the office of Carencro High School, dropping off an attendance form for my French teacher. The radio was on and the secretaries looked stricken. They told me what had just happened, about the President being shot and taken to the hospital. I got really excited as I ran out of the office. I ran back to the classrooms to start telling people and, goddamn, I wanted Reagan to die because if he did, then whenever anyone was asked where they were when Reagan was shot, they'd say, "Well, I was in my classroom when this guy came running in . . ."

I wondered where I should go first and then the obvious answer hit me: Civics class. I mean, where else would you go to tell someone the President's possibly been assassinated? You remember Civics? Remember having an entire course that taught you about your responsibilities as a citizen in the nation? How that wasn't called "indoctrination" because it was actually giving you a life skill by understanding what all those things are that control every aspect of your life? Seems quaint now, no? So I ran into Mr. Nettles's class and interrupted him, just saying, "Someone shot the President," before running out. Mr. Nettles came to the door and shouted at me, "If you're lying, Lee Papa, I'm gonna put your butt in detention."

Too late, though. I was off, man, I was fuckin' Paul Revere, going from class to class, telling everyone, "The President was shot, the President was shot," thinking, shit, at least we'll get out for the rest of the day. Who can study trig when Ronald Reagan's in the hospital? I was going, man, I had a full head of steam, "Reagan's been shot, Reagan's been shot," and then I got to my French class where I opened my mouth; the teacher looked at me and yelled, "En francais!"

Now, who the fuck in French 1 knows the word for "shot," let alone "assassinated"? "Uh, madame, le . . . President . . . est . . . morte." Dead. Sure. Close enough. Madame Bruce looked at me wide-eyed and in Cajun-accented English, said, "The President is dead?"

"Peut-être," I jumped in. Perhaps. And then I ran away to tell more people.

But, no, fucker lived. For another 23 years. We can't escape from Ronald Reagan. We can't escape from the man who can claim Reagan as his true father, George W. Bush. We can't escape from President Obama justifying his policies based on "Well, Reagan did it." We can't ever, ever escape from Ronald Reagan. He set us on the road to damnation and doom.

Here's the deal, oh, dear, sweet fellow Americans: if we continue the direction we're going, we're fucked as a nation. We have become a bloated old drag queen, going through the motions of putting on makeup and feathers, as if that's gonna hide the wrinkles and sags, dancing the same steps for thirty years, shaking it on the stage for the sake of nostalgia and pity cheers. It may be too late to change this path. Better and bigger empires than ours have fallen. And the worst part is that we know what to do. We know what would save us, but we're no longer capable of making such bold leaps. We've been cowed and divided and overfed.

Still, if we were willing to gamble on a big damn strategy, we've gotta be ready to go to war in 2012. And here's a half-dozen ideas, ones that I think are just obvious, starting with how to afford to be a country anymore:

1. Raise taxes. The U.S. currently has one of the lowest tax rates in the world. The very notion that we would want to cut taxes on the wealthy is ludicrous: remember, the rich have accountants who help them avoid paying a good chunk of what they owe, through (most of the time) perfectly legal means. Bring all income taxes back to the levels of the 1990s. And then jack 'em up on the highest brackets. You wanna call it "wealth redistribution"? Fine. I'll call it "running the nation like rational fucking human beings and not selfish pricks who think they can have everything for nothing."

2. End the war(s). First off, let's bottom line this shit: the Iraq war was a hubristic joke to test out a political theory that a bunch of neocon geeks concocted after sucking down single malt Scotch and banging Palestinian prostitutes. The Afghanistan war was always a joke, even when most liberals saw it as the good one. The attacks of September 11, 2001 were the actions of an organization of a couple hundred goatfucking cavedwellers being manipulated by deranged religious leaders and rich assholes. It was a James Bond villain plot that James Bond didn't stop. Stopping Al-Qaeda was always an intelligence matter, with minimal military involvement. But now we're there, we're told, because the Taliban are a bunch of goatfucking cavedwellers who treat people like shit. Welcome to the world. Fuck morality here for a moment. We can't afford to be at war. We need to rebuild Detroit and New Orleans. And protecting the populations of a nation from jerk-off leaders ought to fall to the United Nations or a larger NATO operation, not primarily to us.

3. Legalize pot. You wanna make shitloads of money? You wanna make the nation safer by freeing up the police? You wanna save a ton by emptying the prisons? You wanna put a bunch of criminals out of business? I'm no stoner. I don't wake and bake. I'm not sitting here listening to Phish and dreaming of a time when I can smoke a doobie on the streets.[1] It's just simple and it's been simple for a long, long time: pot's here to stay. The decriminalization of marijuana is a no-brainer for states and cities looking to figure out how they can afford their police forces. Legalize it, tax the fuck out of it, penalize people who do stupid shit while on it, and reap a huge financial bounty.

4. Spend the money. And that means federal and state governments spending the money on employing people, not giving huge chunks of it to contractors who then pay sub-contractors who pay sub-sub-contractors and fuck-all is left to actually do what needed to be done in the first place. Universal health care. Infrastructure repair and construction. Massive education reinvestment. We need a new Works Progress Administration, not tax breaks for small business development. It's a massive stimulus to the economy. Citizens need to see that their tax dollars are doing something, and they need to understand that they are part of one big effort to make the country better.

5. Grant amnesty to the illegal immigrants here. The sickening amount of resources devoted to sending mostly law-abiding people back to Mexico is a huge waste. And if you want to end the exploitation of the labor force that provides us with most of our produce, cleans our homes, raises our kids, and makes delicious street tacos for us to enjoy, then the only humane thing to do is to grant amnesty and get people on the path to citizenship. If we were inundated with millions of illegal Swedes, this would have been done years ago.

6. Restore the power of unions in America. That means the Congress needs to pass things like the Employee Free Choice Act, which will

---

1 But getting high and listening to Radiohead while fucking another person or two? Now that's fun.

jump start unionization again. Democrats need to harness the selfishness of workers, and the chance for higher wages and greater benefits is an awesome way to start. Concurrently, union workers need to be willing to act, going on sympathy strikes for, say, the right of Wal-Mart workers to organize.

There ya go. Maybe a couple of them will be done at some point. Most won't. But isn't it better to end a book with blind optimism rather than outright despair? That's so woefully and wonderfully American. Oh, yeah, I forgot. Who's going to be the 2012 nominee? Fuck, I don't know. John Thune? Chris Christie? **RP**

BIBLIOGRAPHY

(Works are listed in order used. Any works cited in the text are not cited here.)

Radio Ad from the 1930s
"Political Notes: Republican Drama." *Time*, January 27, 1936.

How to Make Something Completely Innocuous Appear Totally Evil
"List of Obama Czars." *The Glenn Beck Program*. Premiere Radio Networks. August 21, 2009.
  http://www.glennbeck.com/content/articles/article/198/29391/.
Matthis, Nancy. "The Compleat List of Czars." *American Daughter Media Center*. August 3, 2009.
  http://frontpage.americandaughter.com/?p=2385.
All Reagan appointee references come from documents in the papers of Ronald Reagan at the American Presidency Project.
  http://www.presidency.ucsb.edu/

Jim DeMint
"Jim DeMint on the Issues."
  http://www.issues2000.org/House/Jim_DeMint.htm
Kennedy, Dan. "Axis of Evil." *Boston Phoenix*, November 12 -18, 2004.
DeMint, Jim. "Abstinence Education Enables Educated Decisions." April 28, 2008.
  http://demint.senate.gov
DeMint, Jim. "Congress Must Protect Unborn in Considering Health Care Reform." October 22, 2009.
  http://demint.senate.gov/
DeMint, Jim. "It's going to keep snowing in DC until Al Gore cries 'uncle'," February 9, 2010.
  http://twitter.com/jimdemint/status/8863771523

Founding Fathers Fun Time
Beck, Glenn. "Glenn's Fav Founding Father." *The Glenn Beck Program*. Premiere Radio Networks, July 18, 2008.
  http://www.glennbeck.com/content/articles/article/198/12587/.
Franklin, Benjamin. *The Autobiography and Other Writings*. New York, NY: Penguin, 2008. 68.

Great Moments in Wealth Redistribution #1

Reagan, Ronald. "Radio Address to the Nation on Proposed Legislation for a Highway and Bridge Repair Program." November 27, 1982. http://www.presidency.ucsb.edu/ws/index.php?pid=42038

Mike Pence

Mike Pence's Congressional home page. http://mikepence.house.gov/

Burton, Danielle. "What You Didn't Know About Rep. Mike Pence of Indiana." *U.S. News and World Report*, November 15, 2006. http://www.usnews.com/usnews/news/articles/061115/15pencefacts.htm

Pence, Mike. "Border Security and Immigration: Building a Principled Consensus for Reform." The Heritage Foundation, June 2, 2006. http://www.heritage.org/Research/Lecture/Border-Security-and Immigration-Building-a-Principled-Consensus-for-Reform

"Mike Pence for President 2012." April 17, 2009. http://www.facebook.com/group.php?gid=59363348372

"As Washington opens spigots for Katrina relief, protests mount." Agence France-Presse, September 19, 2005.

Pence, Mike. "The President's Troubling Trend on the World Stage." *Human Events*, September 29, 2009.

Jeb Bush

Quinn, Justin. "A Biography of Florida Governor Jeb Bush." http://usconservatives.about.com/od/champions/p/A-Biography-Of-Florida-Governor-Jeb-Bush.htm

Farrington, Brendan. "Florida Governor Dedicates Faith-Based Prison." AP, December 24, 2003.

Hannigan, Joni B. "Schiavo family spends day with Terri; Lieberman backs Gov. Bush." *Florida Baptist Witness*, October 24, 2003. http://www.gofbw.com/news.asp?ID=1712

Kleindienst, Linda. "The Jeb Bush Era Ends in Florida." *Washington Post*, January 5, 2007.

Rick Santorum

Newall, Mike. "The Path of the Righteous Man." Washington *City Paper*, September 29-October 5, 2005.

Rick Santorum (continued)

Leibovich, Mark. "Father First, Senator Second." *Washington Post*, April 18, 2005.

"Santorum Exposed."
http://www.santorumexposed.com/pages/issues/issues-tax.php

Laughlin, Sean. "Santorum under fire for comments on homosexuality." CNN, April 22, 2003.
http://www.cnn.com/2003/ALLPOLITICS/04/22/santorum.gays/

"George Stephanopoulos Interviews Sen. Rick Santorum." *Think Progress*, July 31, 2005. http://thinkprogress.org/santorum-this-week/

"Report: Hundreds of WMDs Found in Iraq." Fox News, June 22, 2006.
http://web.archive.org/web/20080424081106/http:/www.foxnews.com/story 0,2933,200499,00.html

Mike Huckabee

On The Issues, "Mike Huckabee on Health Care."
http://www.ontheissues.org/2008/Mike_Huckabee_Health_Care.htm

Huckabee, Mike. *Character IS the Issue: How People with Integrity Can Revolutionize America*. New York: B&H Books, 1997.

Arkansas Kids First website.
http://www.arkidsfirst.com

"Morris claimed Huckabee's 'refusal to indulge in negative advertising. show[ed] his strength under fire' – after deriding his actions on anti-Romney as 'stupid'." *Media Matters*, January 04, 2008.
http://mediamatters.org/research/200801040007

"Fox News contributor Mike Huckabee falsely claimed 'not one drop of oil was spilled' during Hurricane Katrina." *Media Matters*, June 27, 2008.
http://mediamatters.org/research 200806270005

2002 AR Gubernatorial National Political Awareness Test Nov 1, 2002

"All-American Presidential Forum." PBS, Sept. 27, 2007.

Founding Fathers Fun Time

"This Week Transcript: Former Vice President Dick Cheney." ABC News, Febuary 14, 2010.
http://abcnews.go.com/ThisWeek/week-transcript-vice-president-dick-cheney/story?id=9818034&page=3

Lea, Russell M. *A Hero and a Spy: the Revolutionary War Correspondence of Benedict Arnold*. Westminster, Md.: Heritage Books, 2006.

The Easiest Takedown of Our Detention Policy

The White House Archives. "The Vice President Appears on ABC's This Week." January 27, 2002.

http://georgewbush-whitehouse.archives.gov/vicepresident/news-speeches/speeches/vp20020127.html

GlobalSecurity.org. "Guantanamo Bay Detainees."

http://www.globalsecurity.org/military/facility/guantanamo-bay_detainees.htm.

(All dates and numbers for detainee release come from this website.)

"Blair, Bush defend war." CNN, July 17, 2003.

http://www.cnn.com/2003/US/07/17/blair/index.html

Porteus, Liza. "To Close or Not to Close Gitmo?" Fox News. July 15, 2005.

http://www.foxnews.com/story/0,2933,159521,00.html

"Transcript: Cheney Defends Hard Line Tactics." ABC News, December 16, 2008.

http://abcnews.go.com/Politics/story?id=6464697&page=1

The White House Archives. "Live Interview of the Vice President by Bill Bennett, Morning in America." January 13, 2009.

http://georgewbush-whitehouse.archives.gov/news/releases/2009/01/20090113.html

"'This Week' Transcript: Panetta." ABC News, June 27, 2010.

http://abcnews.go.com/ThisWeek/week-transcript-panetta/story?id=11025299&page=2

Halperin, Mark. "Excerpts from Cheney on Fox Business Network." *Time*, May 12, 2009.

http://thepage.time.com/excerpts-from-cheney-on-fox-business-network/

The Tea Party: Howard Dean's Sloppy Seconds

Jenkins, Sally. "Return of the Angry Man." *The Washington Post*, July 3, 2005, W 08.

"Howard Dean's remarks at the Democratic convention." *USA Today*, June 27, 2004.

"Transcript: Glenn Beck." CNN, June 21, 2007.

http://transcripts.cnn.com/TRANSCRIPTS/0706/21/gb.01.html

Three Obama Urban Legends...

Ku Klux Klan. "Ku Klux Klan Does Not Endorse Barack Obama for President." February 28, 2009. http://www.kkk.bz/pressreleasebarak222008.pdf

NRA. "Rumor Control–Debunking the Latest Legends." February 6, 2009. http://www.nraila.org/legislation/federal/read.aspx?id=4404

Founding Fathers Fun Time

Washington, George. *Writings*. John H. Rhodehamel. New York: Library of America, 1997.

Sarah Palin

Bell, Tom. "Alaskans line up for a whiff of Ivana." *Anchorage Daily News*, April 3, 1996

Mitchell, Greg. "Archives of Alaska Papers Reveal Disturbing – And Goofy – Details from Palin's Past." *Editor and Publisher*, September 3, 2008. http://www.editorandpublisher.com/eandp/search/article_display. jsp?vnu_content_id=1003845449

Guntzel, Jeff Severns. "While Biden issued warnings in Kosovo, Palin wept in a Wal-Mart." *Minnesota Independent*, September 29, 2008.

Kane, Paul. "Palin's Small Alaska Town Secured Big Federal Funds." *The Washington Post*, September 2, 2008.

Newton-Small, Jay. "Why Sarah Palin Quit: The Five Best Explanations." *Time*, July 6, 2009.

Palin-Parnell Campaign Booklet. *New Energy for Alaska*. November 3, 2006.

MacGillis, Alec. "As Mayor of Wasilla, Palin Cut Own Duties, Left Trail of Bad Blood." *Washington Post*, September 14, 2009. A1.

Palin, Sarah. *Going Rogue: An American Life*. New York: Harper-Collins, 2009.

"Palin stepping down this month." CNN, July 03, 2009. http://articles.cnn.com/2009-07-03/politics/palin_1_sarah-palin-randy-ruedrich-re-election-plans?_s=PM:POLITICS

Montopoli, Brian. "Sarah Palin Fox News Show Gets Mixed Reviews." CBS News, April 2, 2010. http://www.cbsnews.com/8301-503544_162-20001655-503544.html

The Source of All Evil: Karl Rove

DuBose, Lou, Jan Reid, and Carl M. Cannon. *Boy Genius: Karl Rove, the Brains Behind the Remarkable Political Triumph of George W. Bush*. Washington, D.C.: Public Affairs, 2003.

Moore, James, and Wayne Slater. *Bush's Brain: How Karl Rove Made George W. Bush Presidential*. New York: Wiley, 2003.

Rove, Karl. *Courage and Consequence: My Life as a Conservative in the Fight*. New York: Threshold, 2010.

Grieder, William. *Who Will Tell the People: The Betrayal of American Democracy*. New York: Simon and Schuster, 1993.

Six Conservative Talk Radio Hosts You Might Not Know
Michael Berry

Mendoza, Moises. "Talk show host Michael Berry under fire for mosque bomb remark." KHOU-TV, Houston, TX. May 28, 2010. http://www.khou.com/news/Talk-show-host-Michael-Berry-under-fire-for-mosque-bomb-remark-95129684.html

Michael Berry Home Page. http://ktrh.com/pages/michaelberry.html

Mike DelGiorno

Michael DelGiorno Sucks. http://www.michaeldelgiornosucks.com

Lassek, P.J. "Radio station retracts remarks." *Tulsa World*, December 20, 2007.

"Radio Host Banished From Casinos." *Casino City Times*, August 15, 2006.

Michael DelGiorno page. 99WTN, Nashville, TN. http://www.997wtn.com/Onair/MichaelDelgiorno/tabid/172/Default.aspx

Bates, Michael D. "Cognitive Dissonance, Personified." *Urban Tulsa Weekly*, April 25, 2007.

DelGiorno, Michael. *Standing Up for What's Right*. Dallas: Brown Books, 2004.

Roger Hedgecock

Maass, Dave. "Conservative DJ Roger Hedgecock Says Dems 'Crave Dead Miners'." *Huffington Post*, April 6, 2010. http://www.huffingtonpost.com/dave-maass/conservative-dj-roger-hed_b_527832.html

"Limbaugh sub host claimed Obama-McCain incident shows 'how Democrats treat African-Americans' officeholders: '[T]hey get put back on the plantation'." *Media Matters*, February 10, 2006. http://mediamatters.org/mmtv/200602100016

"Hedgecock baselessly compared Baghdad's violent death rate to D.C.'s." *Media Matters*, November 29, 2006. http://mediamatters.org/research/200611300002

"Limbaugh substitute host: Rush was right on prison abuse – this is like college; this is like fraternities.'" *Media Matters*, May 18, 2004.
http://mediamatters.org/research/200405180001

Bob Lonsberry

Lonsberry, Bob. "Who Is This Guy?" September 8, 2010.
http://www.lonsberry.com/bio.cfm

Lonsberry, Bob. "Welfare Is a Cancer." May 26, 2010.
http://www.boblonsberry.com/writings.cfm?story=2881&go=4

Dean-Kawamura, Ben. "Rochester's Anti-Racist Movement Visits WHAM." *Rochester Indy Media*, June 27, 2008.
http://rochester.indymedia.org/newswire/display/21444/index.php

"Outrage at the Outrageous in Our Little Town." *Rochester City Newspaper*, October 1, 2003.

Lonsberry, Bob. "A Lonsberry Life." February 26, 2010.
http://www.boblonsberry.com/writings.cfm?story=2818&go=4

Dean-Kawamura, Ben. "Lonsberry's Racist, Sexist and Classist remarks." *Rochester Indy Media*, June 27, 2008.
http://rochester.indymedia.org/newswire/display/21443/index.php

Janet Parshall

Janet Parshall Home Page.
http://www.moodyradio.org/inthemarketwithjanetparshall/

"Parshall suggested Matthew Shepard's lifestyle was responsible for his murder, called gay adoption 'state-sanctioned child abuse'." *MMFA*, January 18, 2006.
http://mediamatters.org/mmtv/200601190001

Brian Sussman

Sussman, Brian. 'My "Official' Auto-Biography." 2009.
http://www.godgunsandgold.com/about.html

Brian Sussman's Twitter feed.
http://twitter.com/thesussman

Sussman, Brian. *Climategate: A Veteran Meteorologist Exposes the Global Warming Scam*. Washington, D.C.: WND Books, 2010.

"Brian Sussman from KSFO 560AM at HUGE Pleasanton Tea Party (Part 1)." Video. http://www.youtube.com/watch?v=emAvn5afEy8

Newt Gingrich

Romano, Lois. "Newt Gingrich, Maverick on the Hill: The New Right's Abrasive Point Man Talks of Changing His Tone and Tactics." *Washington Post*, January 3, 1985. B1.

Clinton, Hillary R.. *Living History*. New York: Simon & Schuster, 2003.

"The Contract with America." 1994.
    http://www.house.gov/house/Contract/CONTRACT.html

"Gingrich comment on shutdown labeled 'bizarre' by White House." CNN, November 16, 1995.
    http://www.cnn.com/US/9511/debt_limit/11-16/budget_gingrich/

Yang, John E.. "House Reprimands, Penalizes Speaker." *Washington Post*, January 22 1997.

Talbot, Stephen. "Newt's Glass House." *Salon*, Aug. 28, 1998.
    http://www.salon.com/news/1998/08/28news.html

Five Times Ann Coulter Called for People to Die or Mocked the Dead

1. *The O'Reilly Factor*. Fox News, June 22, 2009.

2. *Hannity*. Fox News, August 12, 2009.

3. "That Was No Lady - That Was My Husband." June 28, 2007 column.

4. *Good Morning, America*. ABC, June 25, 2007.

5. "The Party of Ideas." November 20, 2003 column.

Haley Barbour

Raines, Howell. "Age Issue Is Focus of Mississippi Race." *New York Times*, October 20, 1982.

Ross, Brian. "Former Tobacco Lobbyist Turned Governor Kills Statewide Anti-Smoking Program." ABC News, December 4, 2006.
    http://blogs.abcnews.com/theblotter/2006/12/former_tobacco_.html

Lynch, Cameron. "The Case for Haley Barbour in the 2012 Presidential Race." *U.S. News and World Report*, March 30, 2010.

"Giuliani: Corruption-Laden Haley Barbour 'On The Top Of Everybody's List' For VP." *Think Progress*, September 5, 2007.
    http://thinkprogress.org/2007/09/05/giuliani-barbour/

Office of the Governor. "Governor Haley Barbour Announces Extension of Temporary Housing Program." Press release. January 19, 2007.
    http://www.governorbarbour.com/recovery/news/2007/jan/
    pr.HousingProgramExt.htm

Haley Barbour (continued)

Fang, Lee. "As Oil Arrives On MS Beaches, Will Barbour Continue To Praise BP And Mock News Coverage Of The Spill?" *Think Progress*, June 2, 2010. http://thinkprogress.org/2010/06/02/barbour-oil-milkjug/

Tim Pawlenty

Smith, Ben. "I, Pawlenty." *Politico*, August 24, 2010. http://www.politico.com/blogs/bensmith/0810/I_Pawlenty.html

Ostermeier, Eric. "Will Minnesotans Elect a Plurality-Winning Governor for a 4th Straight Cycle?" *Smart Politics*, June 6, 2010. http://blog.lib.umn.edu/cspg/smartpolitics/2010/06/will_minnesotans_elect_a_plura.php

Mosedale, Mike. "Secrets and Lies." *Minneapolis City Pages*, July 23, 2003. 16-18.

Lopez, Patricia. "Gas tax increase appears certain." *Minneapolis Star-Tribune*, August 3, 2007.

Birkey, Andy. "Critics call Pawlenty's Abortion Recovery Month 'Pure Politics'." *Minnesota Independent*, April 12, 2010.

It Took Katrina to Prove That Liberals Were Right All Along

Eckholm, Erik. "Last Year's Poverty Rate Was Highest in 12 Years." *The New York Times*, September 10, 2009, A12.

Poverty data from the United States Census Office: http://www.census.gov/hhes/www/poverty/poverty.html

Sokolove, Michael. "The Believer." *The New York Times*, May 22, 2005.

Johnson, Lyndon B. "The Great Society." May 22, 1964. http://www.americanrhetoric.com/speeches/lbjthegreatsociety.htm

Califano, Jr., Joseph A.. "What Was Really Great About the Great Society." *Washington Monthly*, October 1999.

Reagan, Ronald. *The Creative Society: Some Comments on Problems Facing America*. New York: Devin-Adair, 1968.

Miller, John. "Ronald Reagan's Legacy." *Dollars and Sense* 254 (July/August 2004).

Bobby Jindal

Scheets, Gary. "Name game can have racial tinge." Nola.com, May 28, 2007. http://blog.nola.com/topnews/2007/05/name-game_can_have_racial_ting.html

Jindal, Bobby. "Physical Dimensions of Spiritual Warfare." *New Oxford Review*, 61, No. 10 (December 1994).

Hasten, Mike. "Governor's race becomes a labor vs. business battle." *The Town Talk*, September 19, 2007.

"Rush Limbaugh defends Bobby Jindal." Video.
http://www.youtube.com/watch?v=bTR4wqDT4I4

Shea, Dan. "1st Indian-American governor in U.S. vows 'fresh start' for La." *New Orleans Times-Picayune*, October 21, 2007.

Altman, Alex. "What Do Volcano Monitors Do?" *Time*, February 27, 2009.
http://www.time.com/time/health/article/0,8599,1882069,00.html

Scott, Robert T.. "Gov. Jindal says he's still awaiting specific corporate, federal plan for oil spill response." *Times-Picayune*, April 29, 2010.

Worst Family

Cheney, Lynne. *Telling the Truth: Why Our Culture and Our Country Have Stopped Making Sense—and What We Can Do About It.* New York: Simon and Schuster, 1995.

Cheney, Lynne, and Robin Preiss Glasser. *America: A Patriotic Primer.* New York: Simon and Schuster Children's Publishing, 2002.

"State Department Post for Cheney Daughter." *The New York Times*, March 2, 2002.

Cheney, Mary. *Now It's My Turn: A Daughter's Chronicle of Political Life.* New York: Pocket Books, 2006.

Engelberg, Stephen. "C.I.A. Has $100 Million, a Point to Prove." *The New York Times*, November 2, 1986.

Glenn Beck Is the New Martin Luther King (in Hell)

Beck, Glenn. "Time to Be Heard: The Content of Character." *Glenn Beck.* Fox News, January 15, 2010.
http://www.foxnews.com/story/0,2933,583143,00.html

Beck, Glenn. "What is 'Social Justice'?" *Glenn Beck.* Fox News, March 24, 2010.
http://www.glennbeck.com/content/articles/article/198/38320/

Thomas Paine Would Die For Your Sins

Fruchtman, Jack. *Thomas Paine: Apostle of Freedom.* New York: Four Walls Eight Windows, 1994.

Thomas Paine Would Die For Your Sins (continued)

Hitchens, Christopher. *Thomas Paine's* Rights of Man: *A Biography*. New York: Atlantic Monthly Press, 2006.

Paine, Thomas. *Paine: Collected Writings*. New York: Library of America, 1995.